QUIZ
BOOK

QUIZ
BOOK

Fun and games with *The Archers*

HEDLI NIKLAUS AND TREVOR HARRISON

BOOKS

Dedicated to Annette, Norman and Agnes, Leon, Nick and Kate, –
our families – who between them managed to answer all our
questions and solve the puzzles so that we could write this book.
We hope our listeners and readers will be able to do the same!

Published in Great Britain by BBC Books, BBC Worldwide,
Woodlands, 80 Wood Lane, London W12 0TT
First published 2003
Copyright © Hedli Niklaus and Trevor Harrison 2003
The moral right of the authors have been asserted

ISBN 0 563 48876 X

Commissioning Editor: Emma Shackleton
Project Editor: Cath Harries
Design Manager: Sarah Ponder
Designer: Diane Clouting
Production Controller: Belinda Rapley

Set in AGaramond by BBC Worldwide Limited
Printed and bound in Great Britain by Mackays of Chatham
Jacket printed by Belmont Press

Official *Archers* Website: www.bbc.co.uk/radio4/archers
for *Archers* episodes in Real Audio, including an audio archive of the
last seven days. The site also features daily plot synopses, news,
information, a map of Ambridge, quizzes and chat.

Official Fan Club: Archers Addicts 0121 683 1951
Web site: www.archers-addicts.com

INTRODUCTION

Being part of *The Archers* is a fascinating experience.
It's not just that we're involved in the day-to-day
storylines, recording episodes in our Birmingham
studios, and wondering what our characters will be up
to next, but that we touch upon a whole world outside
Ambridge, the one created by our loyal listeners. For
some, *The Archers* is more than a radio programme, it
is a way of life.

Over the years we've had the chance to meet our
listeners and hear their views. They certainly know
their subject! Sometimes they remember facts we never
even knew… "But Phil Archer prefers his eggs
boiled!"… "Of course Brian Aldridge reads G A
Henty." Our audience has definitely tested our
knowledge of *The Archers*!

When Archers Addicts, the official fan club for
the programme, holds events we find The Bull Pub
Quizzes and 'Brain of Borchester' contests are
especially popular. The fans pit their wits against each
other (and us!) with relish. Trevor developed into a
whiz at concocting tricky questions, with a dash of
gentle humour, while Hedli became adept at checking
out the answers and adding the occasional tortuous
twist of her own. It seemed natural for us to work
together and extend the fun for fans by putting
together our very own *Archers Quiz Book*.

The book took on a life of its own as we developed all sorts of ideas. We wanted the book to have something for everyone, for listeners who have tuned in from 1951 to those who've just started; a book that you could read at bedtime, take on holiday, enjoy when travelling or even use for a social *Archers* evening with friends and family. And then we thought, why just quizzes, why not include puzzles and word searches?

Hedli and daughter Kate spent hours of pleasurable research amongst puzzle books of all types, then created their own puzzles all tinged with an Ambridge flavour. Meanwhile Trevor and his wife Annette, who live in the middle of 'Borsetshire' went straight to its heart. He searched through many glorious old countryside books, chatted to real country folk like 'Bert Fry', discovering old country proverbs and names for country places. All these influences are reflected in the book so that it will appeal to people who love a country way of life as well as *The Archers*.

The book is divided into the four sections with quizzes and puzzles appropriate to each of the four seasons and Ambridge events it celebrates.

We truly hope that you will have as much pleasure in reading our book and solving the quizzes and puzzles as we have had writing it. Thank you to *The Archers* and the countryside for letting us pass on some of your wonders.

Hedli Niklaus and Trevor Harrison, July 2003

SPRING

SPRINGING BACK TO LIFE

With the arrival of spring the countryside comes alive and it's a time for new beginnings. Shula knows this better than anyone. Have you kept pace with all the changes in Shula's life?

1 Who is Shula's twin?

2 What does Shula do for the church?

3 What is the name of the Estate Agents where Shula started work as an office junior?

ⓐ Snatch, Baggy & Foster
ⓑ Rodway & Watson
ⓒ Underwoods
ⓓ Holmes and Watson

4 What happened to Shula when she was with Simon Parker in a Netherbourne cornfield?

ⓐ Broke her leg
ⓑ Found a crop circle
ⓒ Lost her purse
ⓓ Lost her innocence

5 In 1987 Mark and Shula thought she might be pregnant as she was craving what?

ⓐ Plums
ⓑ Peanut butter
ⓒ Lager and lime
ⓓ Radio 4

6 Mark Hebden was a local councillor for which party?

ⓐ Conservative
ⓑ Labour
ⓒ Social Democrat
ⓓ Green

answers ➜ page 31

7 What did Shula buy from her aunt in 2001?

ⓐ Very rare necklace
ⓑ Snooker table for Alistair
ⓒ Second-hand bike
ⓓ Riding school

8 In 1998 who did Shula find herself attracted to?

ⓐ Cameron Fraser
ⓑ Richard Locke
ⓒ Clive Horrobin
ⓓ Robert Snell

9 What was Mark Hebden's profession?

ⓐ Doctor
ⓑ Vet
ⓒ Solicitor
ⓓ Vicar

10 In what year was Daniel born?

ⓐ 1996
ⓑ 1984
ⓒ 2002
ⓓ 1994

11 What did Daniel call a picture he drew of Alistair?

ⓐ My dad
ⓑ A funny man
ⓒ Silly billy
ⓓ My friend

12 What sort of management course did Lilian Bellamy advise Shula to attend?

ⓐ Man management
ⓑ Tree management
ⓒ Home management
ⓓ Horse management

answers ➜ page 31

LOVE IS IN THE AIR

From church bells, orange blossom, love and marriage to affairs,
heartbreak and divorce. How much do you know about the
intimate side of Ambridge life?

1 Can you name Phil Archer's first wife?

2 Who was Neil Carter's best man?

3 With whom did policeman Dave Barry have an affair?

4 Which couple got married on 12 May 2000?

5 David Archer was engaged in 1986 – who was the lucky girl?

a *Mandy Beesborough*
b *Sophie Barlow*
c *Dolly Treadgold*
d *Caroline Bone*

**6 What did a young Nigel Pargetter once wear to take Elizabeth
Archer back to school?**

a *Cap and gown*
b *Suit of armour*
c *Pair of boxer shorts*
d *His trademark gorilla suit*

7 Who was the first husband of Jolene Perks?

a *Wayne Tucson*
b *Snatch Foster*
c *Baggy*
d *Wayne Foley*

8 Walter Gabriel once actually proposed, but to whom?

a *Christine Archer*
b *Doris Forrest*
c *Polly Perkins*
d *Polly Perks*

answers ➔ page 31

9 Who was Penelope Radford?

a *Jack Woolley's first wife*
b *One of Nigel Pargetter's business associates*
c *One of Nelson Gabriel's up-market girlfriends*
d *One of Walter Gabriel's down-market girlfriends*

10 Who was married on 16 November 1957?

11 With whom did Janet Fisher fall in love?

a *Cyril Hood*
b *Neil Carter*
c *The Vicar of Dibley*
d *Tim Hathaway*

A FARMER'S SQUARE

Fit the answers to the clues into the square.
The words read the same down as across

	1	2	3	4
1				
2				
3				
4				

1 *220 yards × 22 yards of farmland*
2 *A bird that needs scaring*
3 *Doris Archer's favourite flower*
4 *Woolly versions of you!*

answers ➜ page 32

ALL CREATURES GREAT AND SMALL

Spring is brimming with new life at Brookfield and the children have made a list of seven of the creatures they've spotted on the farm. Below are their official names – what are they?

1 Mountain Bulinis

a Hereford bull
b Butterfly
c Snail found on the trunks of certain trees
d Bird which visits Britain in Spring

2 Devil's Coach Horse

a West Country name for a rat
b Beetle about 1" long
c Small fish that bites
d Dragon fly

3 Painted Lady

a Female dormouse
b Jolene
c Butterfly
d Starling

4 Common Tern

a Low flying bat
b Dross gig
c Frog
d Sea and inland water bird

5 Flittermouse

a Bat
b Water rat
c Hamster
d Young hare

6 Ringed Snake

a Adder
b Slow worm
c Grass snake
d Simon Pemberton

7 Minnow

a Cat
b Small cow
c Bird
d Fish

answers → page 32

RIDDLE ME REE

My first is in SUNSHINE yet isn't in HEAT

My second is in RAINING but never in SLEET

My third is in STORM though it isn't in THUNDER

My fourth is in BLOOMING and also in BLUNDER

My fifth is not in STRAW but you'll find it in HAY

My sixth is found in PASSION and also in LAY

My seventh is not in DAYTIME – you'll find it in NIGHT

My whole is a person who sets fires alight

answers ➜ page 32

'IT'S OFF TO WORK THEY GO'

The days are getting longer and everyone is busy
(even if one or two are busy doing nothing, as usual!)
See if you know who does what in Ambridge.

1 Who is the landlady of The Bull?

2 Who delivers the milk?

3 Who is head gardener at Lower Loxley?

a *Titchmarsh*   b *Titcombe*
c *Travers-Macy*   d *Tommy Tucker*

4 Who is housekeeper at Lower Loxley?

a *Mrs Blossom*   b *Mrs Fry*
c *Mrs Pritchard*   d *Mrs Pugsley*

5 Who works at Brookfield Farm?

a *Snatch Foster*   b *David Archer*
c *Emma Carter*   d *Nobody*

6 Who is a builder?

a *Jason*   b *Odysseus*
c *Cyril Hood*   d *Jamie Perks*

7 Who is Brian Aldridge's deputy at Home Farm?

a *Greg Turner*   b *Debbie Travers-Macy*
c *William Grundy*   d *Tim Hathaway*

8 Who is Jack Woolley's chauffeur?

a *Higgs*   b *Haggis*
c *Mike Tucker*   d *Ed Grundy*

answers → page 32

SPRING CHICKENS

Let's see how much you know about the younger generation in *The Archers* – some of them you have heard and some you have not!

1 Who was born just before midnight on 20 July 1995?

- *a* Freddie Pargetter
- *b* Gerald Pargetter
- *c* Jazzer
- *d* Jamie Perks

2 Who is one of Phoebe Aldridge's grandmothers?

- *a* Betty Tucker
- *b* Pat Archer
- *c* Jill Archer
- *d* Peggy Woolley

3 Who shares the same birthday as young Ben Archer?

- *a* Neil Carter
- *b* Tony Archer
- *c* Eddie Grundy
- *d* David Archer

4 Who was conceived through an IVF programme?

- *a* Philippa Archer
- *b* Daniel Hebden Lloyd
- *c* Ed Grundy
- *d* Lily Pargetter

5 What is the name of Kenton Archer's daughter?

- *a* Lucy
- *b* Sophie
- *c* Fallon
- *d* Meriel

6 Who is aunt to Noluthando Madikane?

- *a* Helen Archer
- *b* Shula Hebden Lloyd
- *c* Alice Aldridge
- *d* Elizabeth Pargetter

7 Who was born with a hare lip?

- *a* Alice Aldridge
- *b* Jamie Perks
- *c* Freddie Pargetter
- *d* Christopher Carter

answers → page 32

WORDSEARCH

LOVE AND MARRIAGE

Celebrate St Valentine's Day with us by remembering the highs
and lows of our favourite Ambridge couples.
Listed below are the clues to the words you'll find in the Wordsearch
reading vertically, horizontally, diagonally and backwards. You'll find
the solutions to the clues upside-down at the foot of the page.
If you're on top form you can also find the hidden word that
describes the force that brought these people together (10).

With whom did Sid share a shower? (6)

What is the name of Jennifer's love-child? (4)

What is the name of Brian's love-child? (Good luck!) (6)

Who was Walter Gabriel's first love? (3, 1)

Ed and Fallon's joke Valentine card united Caroline with whom? (6)

Which long-suffering wife bought her own engagement ring? (7)

Who did Dr Locke betray during his affair with Shula? (4)

What new skill did Mike learn to impress Betty? (7)

What flower did Elizabeth wear in her hair when she married Nigel? (4)

Nelson and Julia kissed at Lower Loxley, but in which room? (8)

What was GI Conn Kotchmar's parting gift to Peggy? (5, 7)

Name the pig who started the Carter romance (5)

In which city did Phil propose to Jill? (10)

What is the title of Julia Pargetter's first romantic novel? (8, 9)

Jolene, Adam, Ruairí, Mrs.P, Oliver, Clarrie, Usha, dancing, rose, ballroom, Zippo
lighter, Pinky, Birmingham, Passion's Plaything

SOLUTIONS TO THE CLUES

answers ➜ page 33

```
R T J O L E N E Y S H M E V L O T S
P Y N K C D A M P K R Q C T A I J R
I J T R E V I L O R E P L D M T P B
Z G P R Y S H P I L S O A B F A I R
B X P A E T O G A S V E R J S R N H
I R O L C G M R I B S N R S P S K M
S R F P H B O E A U I P I K V O Y N
M S I C V M O T P G J O E N M E N G
P K N A G H S H K M N R Y U Z P H R
D I G G U E M G N S U I A J I N O A
Y C A S Z R W I P R A L C Y O E A M
N L H P O U N L R Y D O G N K D T W
H A K P I G A O N L U S I T A O T Y
D N R O L Y S P O D A P U M L D R K
N L U X T F A P E L H B D S P X A N
T O A H N S M I N R V A E R G S C G
J K I E S T L Z W P M L K H O W T P
A N R A L A C I L Y S L I G C S I Y
G E I M B Y E T A T B R A H R I O N
P T D N R H L I R K I O M B E M N Q
I A H I H O P U E R H O D O G X C P
G O W E J M A H G N I M R I B N U S
```

answers → page 33

LYNDA SNELL BRAINTEASER

Spring is a busy time in the countryside but some people are busy
all year round, and we don't just mean the farmers!
Lynda Snell is one of Ambridge's most famous busybodies
but how much do we know about her?

1 Where does Lynda live?

2 Where did Lynda come from (place, that is, not planet!)?

3 What is the name of Lynda's Afghan hound?

ⓐ Persephone   ⓑ Demeter
ⓒ Hermes   ⓓ Mercury

*4 Lynda first got into the Ambridge social scene
by offering to do what?*

ⓐ Fortune-telling at the Village Fete
ⓑ Bungy jumping off the church tower for charity
ⓒ Organising an Ambridge Ghost Walk
ⓓ Giving a talk on 'Panto Productions'

5 From what does Lynda suffer?

ⓐ Delusions of grandeur   ⓑ Migraines
ⓒ Hangovers   ⓓ Hay fever

6 Who 'enjoyed' one of Lynda's aromatherapy massages?

ⓐ Phil Archer   ⓑ Joe Grundy
ⓒ Brian Aldridge   ⓓ The Bishop of Felpersham

*7 Which of Lynda's productions received a bitchy review
by Larry Lovell?*

ⓐ 'Babes in the Millennium Wood'
ⓑ Her one person show, 'Lynda the Vampire Slayer'
ⓒ 'Babes in the Wood'
ⓓ 'Robin Hood'

answers ➜ page 33

PURPLE PASSAGES

Here's a tale of woe and broken promises. To find out what went
wrong just fill in the blanks, then piece together the sentences.
To make it more difficult there's no punctuation to help you!

WHE□ED□IEA□RIVE□ATA□BRI□GEH□LL

TOHE□PHEAP□LO□ISE□F□RBEI□GSO□A□E

L□NDAHA□MO□EDTHEGAR□EN

OR□A□ENTSANDSNA□PED□RO□SLY

TO□L□TE□HA□EDON□ITS□YOUCA□GO

O□AYH□SAI□CHEE□FUL□YIMO□F

A□TERA□L□HE□ESNOP□ACE□KE□NO□E

answers ➔ page 34

AMBRIDGE SPRING CLEANING

Spring – when a young woman's fancy turns to cleaning . . .
Several well known Ambridge residences are due for a dust down
and it's up to you to decide which ones! See how many clues you
need before you guess the correct 'home sweet homes'.

1 This dwelling . . . .

a *had dry rot in the late 1980s*
b *has a Jacobean fireplace*
c *has 7 acres of woodland*
d *is a Grade II listed building*
e *has an area devoted to rare breeds*

2 This dwelling . . . .

a *was a council property until 1991*
b *was fitted with a neo-Georgian front door by its owners*
c *is one of 12 compact houses*
d *was modernised after it was bought*
e *is lived in by a couple with their 2 children, a boy and a girl*

3 This dwelling . . . .

a *is a picturesque cottage*
b *overlooks the duck pond*
c *was once run as a carrier's business*
d *was bought from a man called Tim Wainwright in 1957*
e *was once home to Nelson Gabriel*

4 This dwelling . . . .

a *stands next to a lake*
b *was once run as a leisure centre*
c *is located in the Grey Gables Country Park*
d *was bought by Charles Grenville in 1959*
e *has been restored by the Landmark Trust for holiday
accommodation.*

answers ➔ page 34

5 This dwelling . . . .

a *is a cottage*
b *was owned by the Archers of Brookfield Farm*
c *stands opposite the Village Green*
d *was where Clarrie Grundy once lived*
e *was crashed into by a lorry in 1999*

6 This dwelling . . . .

a *is a farm*
b *has the largest farmhouse in Ambridge*
c *was built in the 18th century*
d *was once converted into flats*

7 This dwelling . . . .

a *was purchased by a newcomer to Ambridge in 2000*
b *had its plan to run beef cattle delayed by the outbreak of foot and mouth disease in 2001*
c *has its milking parlour destroyed by fire in 1996*
d *had its former occupants evicted in April 2000*

8 This dwelling . . . .

a *has a Welsh slate patio*
b *was flooded in early 2002*
c *was purchased in 1985 for £160,000*
d *has a garden with a low-allergen area*

9 This dwelling . . . .

a *has a thatched roof*
b *had a colony of roosting bats*
c *has a walled garden*
d *is the house that once belonged to Doris Archer*

10 This dwelling . . . .

a *stands on a side road off the Borchester Road*
b *had a burglary take place*
c *was once owned by Lilian Archer*
d *has a solicitor currently living in it*

answers ➔ page 34

THE ARCHERS
AND OTHER ANIMALS

Fashion designer Zandra Rhodes claims her knowledge of brucellosis
was gathered from listening to *The Archers*. See how much you have
learned – listed below are certain creatures that have graced our
farmlands over the years. What kinds of animal are they?

1 What is an Anglo-Nubian?

- *a* New England deer
- *b* Very fierce ferret
- *c* Bloodhound
- *d* Goat

2 What are British Friesians?

- *a* Flock of birds that get very cold in the British winter
- *b* Cattle with a high milk yield
- *c* Cattle only bred for beef
- *d* Sheep that produce a lot of wool

3 Which of the following is a sheep dog?

- *a* Fox hound
- *b* Lesser Spotted Sheep Herder
- *c* Border Collie
- *d* Golden Guernsey

4 What is a Rhode Island Red?

- *a* Bull
- *b* Fowl
- *c* Hunting dog
- *d* Hamster

answers ➜ page 35

5 What is a Kerry Hill?

- *a* Sheep
- *b* Duck
- *c* An imported kangaroo
- *d* Name of a small mound next to Lakey Hill

6 What is a Middle White?

- *a* Grey horse
- *b* Wild rabbit
- *c* Pig
- *d* Boxer dog

7 Complete the following: an Embden . . . . ?

- *a* Lloyd
- *b* Pheasant
- *c* Goose
- *d* Saddleback

8 What animal has a brush?

- *a* Woodland basil
- *b* Fox
- *c* Squirrel
- *d* Rat

9 What are simmentals?

- *a* Deer with bright blue horns
- *b* Oven ready chickens
- *c* Alternative name for natterjacks
- *d* Cattle

10 Which of the following is a plump breasted table bird?

- *a* Donald Duck
- *b* What's Up Duck
- *c* Muscovy Duck
- *d* Crispy Duck

answers ➔ page 35

MIDDLE NAMES

You know everything about *The Archers*, including the names of
all the characters. But do you know their full names?
See how many you can guess!

1 Tony Archer

a *Frederick Anthony Archer*
b *Anthony William Daniel Archer*
c *Anthony Philip Doris Archer*
d *Anthony Jeffrey Archer*

2 Freddie Pargetter

a *Frederick Hugo Pargetter*
b *Frederick Cameron Pargetter*
c *Frederick Daniel Pargetter*
d *Frederick Nigel Pargetter*

3 Eddie Grundy

a *Edward Brian Grundy*
b *Edward Joseph Grundy*
c *Edward George Grundy*
d *Edward Bert Grundy*

4 David Archer

a *David Ivan Archer*
b *David Daniel Archer*
c *Phillip David Archer*
d *David Thomas Archer*

5 Alice Aldridge

a *Alice Elizabeth Aldridge*
b *Alice Margaret Aldridge*
c *Alice Anne Aldridge*
d *Alice Zoe Aldridge*

answers ➜ page 35

6 Tom Forrest

a *Thomas Robin Forrest*
b *Thomas William Forrest*
c *Thomas Harry Forrest*
d *Thomas Hardy Forrest*

7 Phil Archer

a *Philip Nelson Archer*
b *Philip Thomas Archer*
c *Philip Walter Archer*
d *Philip Daniel Archer*

8 Philippa Archer

a *Philippa Daisy Archer*
b *Philippa Lily Archer*
c *Philippa Rose Archer*
d *Philippa Petunia Archer*

TEA AT LOWER LOXLEY

It's time for tea! Can you spot the items on the menu at the Orangery Café at Lower Loxley hidden within the sentences? For example: "Here's TO A STar" said Nigel as he raised his glass.

1 "Help! Don't tell me Lynda's organising another jamboree!" cried Phil.

2 Betty asked Susan to scrub under the sink.

3 William reluctantly put the disc on Edward's hi fi.

4 Ruth hated dressing up but Usha found it easy.

5 Brian insisted that Debbie plough the last acre: "Am I your slave?" she demanded, "Do it yourself!".

answers ➜ page 35

HEADS AND TAILS

Can you match heads and tails
to complete these country proverbs?

1 So many fogs in March . . . .

ⓐ . . . makes it easier to nip to The Bull
ⓑ . . . so many frosts in May
ⓒ . . . so many frogs in Spring
ⓓ . . . dampens a man's soul

2 When April blows its horn . . . .

ⓐ . . . our tender lambs are born
ⓑ . . . the winter months are torn
ⓒ . . . it's time to mow the lawn
ⓓ . . . it's good for hay and corn

3 God made the country . . . .

ⓐ . . . man made the land
ⓑ . . . Aldridge made the money
ⓒ . . . man made the town
ⓓ . . . birds make us sing

4 The king's carriage . . . .

ⓐ . . . never catches the deer
ⓑ . . . stops for the sheep
ⓒ . . . never gets stuck in mud
ⓓ . . . can never plough a field

5 It's a long lane . . . .

ⓐ . . . from the Grundy's house to the pub
ⓑ . . . to find your heart's desire
ⓒ . . . that has no turning
ⓓ . . . that has no trees

answers → page 36

6 A woman, a dog and a walnut tree . . . .

a . . . all lived together beneath the sea
b . . . are all a man needs to be happy and free
c . . . will bring luck if, on May day, you kiss all three
d . . . the more you beat them, the better they be

7 You can't see the wood . . . .

a . . . for the trees
b . . . if you wear a big hat
c . . . if your heart's not true
d . . . if night casts its light

8 No bees, no honey, no work . . . .

a . . . it is not funny
b . . . no reason not to shirk
c . . . it's not sunny
d . . . no money

9 A creaking gate . . . .

a . . . needs oiling
b . . . means rain is coming
c . . . lasts longest
d . . . will still keep the ferrets in

10 Fingers were made . . . .

a . . . to tender the soil
b . . . before forks
c . . . to count the cost
d . . . to kneed the bread

11 Wise men in the world are like timber in a hedge . . . .

a . . . few and far between
b . . . they wait until the time is right
c . . . you can't see them until it is too late
d . . . they see everything and say nothing

answers → page 36

WHO ARE THEY?

Spring is the time for new arrivals, and Ambridge has certainly
had its fair share. Below are clues to Ambridge characters
who were not born in the village.
How quickly can you work out who they are?

1 This strong-minded lady . . . .

a *Was born on 6 March 1905*
b *Came from the East End of London*
c *Lived in Manorfield Close*
d *Was Jennifer Aldridge's feared and much loved grandmother*

2 This professional gentleman . . . .

a *Was Marjorie Antrobus's lodger for a while*
b *Lived at Blossom Hill Cottage*
c *Was a member of the Sealed Knot*
d *Was once the village doctor*

3 This married woman . . . .

a *Was born in 1968*
b *Once lodged with Martha Woodford*
c *Addressed the Royal Agricultural Society's 'Young Perspectives'
conference in 1998*
d *Had the maiden name of Pritchard*

4 This young lad . . .

a *Was born when his mother was staying in Great Yarmouth*
b *Almost lost his voice shouting at an Aston Villa football match*
c *Got drunk on home-made apple brandy on his 15th birthday*
d *Once had to do community service*

answers → page 36

5 This clever person . . . .

a *Arrived in Ambridge in 1986*
b *Played a strolling minstrel in 'Babes in the Millennium Wood'*
c *Knows a lot about computers*
d *Was snapped up by the cricket team as a member of the Marylebone Cricket Club (MCC)*

6 This bright young lass . . . .

a *Was born in Penny Hassett*
b *Was married in 1966*
c *Was once the landlady of The Bull*
d *Was killed in 1982 when her car hit a milk tanker*

7 This reliable chap . . . .

a *First came to Ambridge in 1973*
b *Owns a few acres at Willow Farm*
c *Was a feed representative for Borchester Mills*
d *Has a daughter who was injured in a car crash in 2001*

8 This old age pensioner. . . .

a *Was born in 1928*
b *Was a gamekeeper*
c *Plays the cornet*
d *Became chairman of the Parish Council*

9 This young man. . . .

a *Was in Ed Grundy's class at school*
b *Sang in the band Dross*
c *Was born in 1984*
d *Is known by his nickname, but his real name is Jack McCreary*

10 This farm labourer. . . .

a *Was made a church warden*
b *Is a cricket umpire*
c *Likes to think of himself as a bit of a poet*
d *Once had his own column in the Borchster Echo*

answers → page 36

COUNTRY LOVERS?

We all enjoy walking and driving through the countryside in
springtime but how many of us know the old English meanings
of the place names we pass through? Test your knowledge and
find out whether you are a country lover or a country bumpkin!

1 What is a 'dale' ?

2 What is a 'dell' ?

3 What is a 'stead'?

- ⓐ Place
- ⓑ River meadow
- ⓒ Valley
- ⓓ Bridge

4 What is a 'combe' ?

- ⓐ Moat
- ⓑ Colony
- ⓒ Valley
- ⓓ River

5 What is a 'thorpe' ?

- ⓐ Village
- ⓑ Town
- ⓒ City
- ⓓ Country

6 What is the Scottish word for valley?

- ⓐ Glyn
- ⓑ Gill
- ⓒ Gale
- ⓓ Glen

7 What is a 'pont' ?

- ⓐ House
- ⓑ Church
- ⓒ Lamppost
- ⓓ Bridge

8 What is a 'mere' ?

- ⓐ Place for horses
- ⓑ Lake
- ⓒ Home
- ⓓ Coast

9 What is a 'wardine' an old name for?

- ⓐ Pub or inn
- ⓑ Church
- ⓒ Holding or farm
- ⓓ Wedding dinner

answers → page 36

SOLUTIONS

SPRINGING BACK TO LIFE

1   Kenton Archer is Shula's twin brother.

2   Shula is a churchwarden.

3   *b*   Estate Agents Rodway and Watson gave Shula her first real job.

4   *d*   Shula lost her innocence to Simon Parker in a Netherbourne cornfield.

5   *b*   A craving for peanut butter misled Mark and Shula into believing that their dreams were coming true.

6   *c*   Mark Hebden was a candidate for the Social Democrats.

7   *d*   Christine Barford sold her riding school to Shula in 2001.

8   *b*   Richard Locke and Shula had a fling that lost her a friendship with his girlfriend Usha.

9   *c*   Mark Hebden was a solicitor.

10 *d*   Daniel Hebden Lloyd was born in 1994.

11 *a*   Daniel called his drawing 'my dad'.

12 *d*   Lilian recommended Shula to attend a horse management course.

LOVE IS IN THE AIR

1   *The name of Phil Archer's first wife was Grace (neé Fairbrother).*

2   *Eddie Grundy was Neil Carter's best man.*

3   *Dave Barry had an affair with wayward Kathy Perks.*

4   *Simon Gerrard and Debbie Aldridge married on 12 May 2000.*

5   *b*   *Sophie Barlow opted for a career in fashion rather than in farming and broke off her engagement to David Archer in 1986.*

6   *d*   *Nigel Pargetter wore his trademark gorilla suit to take Elizabeth Archer back to school.*

7   *a*   *Jolene was Mrs Wayne Tucson before she married Sid Perks.*

8   *c*   *Walter Gabriel proposed to the only woman who was more than a match for him, Polly Perkins (aka Mrs P). She turned him down.*

9   *c*   *Penelope Radford (played by Angela Rippon) was one of Nelson Gabriel's more up-market girlfriends.*

10   *Phil Archer and Jill Patterson plighted their troth on 16 November 1957.*

11 *d*   *Janet Fisher fell in love with Tim Hathaway.*

SPRING

A FARMER'S SQUARE

1   *220 yards × 22 of farmland is an ACRE.*
2   *A bird that needs scaring is a CROW.*
3   *Doris Archer's favourite flower was a ROSE.*
4   *Woolly versions of you are EWES.*

ALL CREATURES GREAT AND SMALL

1   *c*   A Mountain Bulini is a snail found on the trunk of certain trees.
2   *b*   Devil's Coach Horse is a small beetle.
3   *e*   Painted Lady is a butterfly.
4   *d*   Common Tern is a sea and inland water bird.
5   *a*   Flittermouse is another name for the common bat.
6   *e*   Ringed Snake is another name for a grass snake.
7   *d*   Minnow is a fish.

RIDDLE ME REE

The answer is Siobhan

'IT'S OFF TO WORK THEY GO'

1	Jolene Perks	5	b	David Archer
2	Mike Tucker	6	a	Jason
3 b	Titcombe	7	b	Debbie Gerrard
4 d	Mrs Pugsley	8	a	Higgs

SPRING CHICKENS

1   *d*   Jamie Perks was born just before midnight on the 20 July 1995.
2   *a*   Betty Tucker is one of Phoebe Aldridge's grandmothers.
3   *c*   Eddie Grundy shares the same birthday as young Ben Archer.
4   *b*   Daniel Hebden Lloyd was conceived by IVF.
5   *d*   Meriel is the name of Kenton Archer's daughter.
6   *c*   Alice Aldridge is aunt to Noluthando Madikane.
7   *d*   Christopher Carter was born with a hare lip.

Five or more of these right and you've shown that you're more than a match for the younger generation!

SPRING

WORDSEARCH - LOVE AND MARRIAGE

The hidden word is ATTRACTION

		J	O	L	E	N	E								
												C			
		R	E	V	I	L	O					L		P	
			S									A		I	
				O								R	S	N	
I					R							R	S	K	
	R				E							I		Y	
		I			T		G		O		E				
			A		H			N							
				U	G		S		I						
			S		R	I	P				C			**A**	
		H			L			N		D				**T**	
	A			A	O				A					**T**	
			Y	P				M		D				**R**	
		T		P			B							**A**	
		H		I			A							**C**	
	I			Z	P		L							**T**	
N				S		L								**I**	
G				R		O								**O**	
				O	M		N								
				O											
		M	A	H	G	N	I	M	R	I	B				

LYNDA SNELL BRAINTEASER

1 Ambridge Hall, once home to Laura Archer

2 Sunningdale

3 *c* Hermes – Lynda showed her softer side when she gave a home to the runt of an Afghan litter.

4 *a* Fortune-telling at the Village Fete

5 *d* Hay fever

6 *b* Joe Grundy – he substituted himself for grandson William, much to Lynda's disgust!

7 *a* 'Babes in the Millennium Wood' in 1999. Larry only had one good word to say for it as he'd been ousted from producing it himself. All he mentioned was the over-riding smell of pig muck and the excellence of Jill's costumes!

All seven correct? You know too much! Your name isn't Lynda by any chance?

SPRING

PURPLE PASSAGES

> WHEN EDDIE ARRIVED AT AMBRIDGE HALL
> TO HELP HE APOLOGISED FOR BEING SO LATE.
> LYNDA HAD MOVED THE GARDEN
> ORNAMENTS AND SNAPPED CROSSLY,
> "TOO LATE - I HAVE DONE IT SO YOU CAN GO".
> "OKAY", HE SAID CHEERFULLY, "I'M OFF.".
> AFTER ALL, THERE'S NO PLACE LIKE GNOME.

AMBRIDGE SPRING CLEANING

1 *Lower Loxley Hall – the family seat of the Pargetter family*
2 *No 1, The Green – home of the Carter family*
3 *Honeysuckle Cottage – home to Walter (who died there in 1988) and Nelson Gabriel until Nelson's death in 2001. The Hathaways lived there until they split up in 2002.*
4 *Arkwright Hall – once owned by Jack Woolley until he offered the building to the Landmark Trust in 1999.*
5 *Woodbine Cottage – the Fry residence*
6 *Home Farm – the Aldridges have lived here since Brian Aldridge bought the property from Ralph Bellamy in 1975.*
7 *Grange Farm after the eviction of the Grundys in 2000 retired farmer Oliver Sterling bought the farm from Borchester Land with an accompanying 50 acres.*
8 *Ambridge Hall – now the residence of Robert and Lynda Snell*
9 *Glebe Cottage – Phil and Jill Archer moved into Glebe Cottage in September 2001*
10 *Blossom Hill Cottage – Usha Gupta is the current owner*

Score: How many steps did you take before arriving at the correct solution?

Mainly a's: Congratulations. You clearly live in a stately home and lunch with the Pargetters

Mainly b's: Excellent. You are well to do country folk and have visited Jennifer Aldridge's web site. She will reward you with one of her famous venison dinners.

Mainly c's: Well done. You are extremely rich and belong to all the right clubs. Enjoy a cocktail party with the Woolleys

Mainly d's: Not so good. You'll need to brush up on Ambridge history to hold your own at an Archers coffee morning

Mainly e's: Clearly a newcomer. Clarrie might bake you a consolation cake if you ask her nicely.

Mainly f's: Oh dear. Do you live in Penny Hassett?

SPRING

THE ARCHERS AND OTHER ANIMALS!

1 *d* An Anglo Nubian is a goat. Lynda Snell used to have two, Persephone and Demeter, but Demeter mysteriously disappeared....

2 *b* British Friesians are cattle with a high milk yield.

3 *c* Border collies are still widely used as sheepdogs.

4 *b* Rhode Island Reds are fowls.

5 *a* A Kerry Hill is a breed of sheep.

6 *c* Middle Whites are pigs, a breed especially loved by Phil Archer.

7 *c* It's an Embden Goose (not a Hebden Lloyd!).

8 *b* A fox has a brush.

9 *d* Simmentals are a breed of cattle.

10 *c* Muscovy duck is a plump breasted table bird.

MIDDLE NAMES

1 b *Anthony William Daniel Archer. Tony was the first Archer grandson so had to be called after Dan Archer!*

2 a *Frederick Hugo Pargetter*

3 c *Edward George Grundy. Clarrie called her younger son after Prince Edward.*

4 d *David Thomas Archer*

5 b *Alice Margaret Aldridge*

6 b *Thomas William Forrest. Tom's father was called William.*

7 c *Philip Walter Archer. Philip was given the middle name of Walter after his highly delighted godfather Walter Gabriel.*

8 c *Philippa Rose Archer*

TEA AT LOWER LOXLEY

1 "Help! Don't tell me Lynda's organising another JAMboree!" cried Phil.

2 Betty asked Susan to scruB UNder the sink.

3 William reluctantly put the disSC ON Edward's hifi.

4 Ruth hated dressing up but Usha found iT EAsy.

5 Brian insisted that Debbie polugh the last aCRE "AM I your slave?". she demanded, "Do it yourself!".

HEADS AND TAILS

1 *b* So many frogs in March so many frosts in May.

2 *d* When April blows its horn it's good for hay and corn.

3 *c* God made the country man made the town.

4 *b* The king's carriage stops for the sheep.

5 *c* It's a long lane that has no turning.

6 *d* A woman, a dog and a walnut tree the more you beat them, the better they be

7 *a* You can't see the wood for the trees.

8 *d* No bees, no honey, no work, no money.

9 *c* A creaking gate lasts longest.

10 *b* Fingers were made before forks.

11 *a* Wise men in the world are like timber in a hedge, few and far between.

WHO ARE THEY?

1 *Polly Perkins (aka Mrs.P)*   2 *Doctor Richard Locke*

3 *Ruth Archer*   4 *Edward Grundy (aka Ed)*

5 *Robert Snell*   6 *Polly Perks*

7 *Neil Carter*   8 *George Barford*

9 *Jazzer*   10 *Bert Fry*

Mainly a's: You know too much. You probably know more about The Archers *than your own family. Go out for dinner with your nearest and dearest and re-acquaint yourselves!*

Mainly b's: For the next six months confine listening to the Omnibus only, and take up a hobby.

Mainly c's: Well done. But remind yourself occasionally that the characters aren't real.

Mainly d's: Excellent. You balance real life enjoyment with listening to your favourite radio series.

COUNTRY LOVERS?

1 A dale is an open valley.   2 A dell is a wooded hollow.

3 *a* Stead is a place.   4 *c* Combe is a valley.

5 *a* Thorpe is a small village

6 *d* The Scottish word for valley is a glen.

7 *d* Pont is a bridge.   8 *b* Mere is a lake.

9 *c* Wardine is the name for a holding or farm.

Well done if you've scored over 5. This was a tough quiz, not for townies nor weekenders.

SUMMER

BROOKFIELD FARM
AND THE ARCHER FAMILY

Have you ever enjoyed a farm holiday at Brookfield? Let's see
how much you know about your hosts and their families . . . .

1 Which male member of the Archer family was born in 1896?

*2 Which female, who became an Archer by marriage, was
born in 1890?*

3 Who were Dan Archer's younger brothers?

  a Frank and Ben   *b* Bill and Ben
  c Phil and Ken   *d* Tom and Jack

4 Who was born on St. George's day in 1928?

  a Christine Archer   *b* Margaret (Peggy) Perkins
  c Phil Archer   *d* John (Jack) Archer

5 Name George Fairbrother's only daughter

  a Pru   *b* Doris
  c Grace   *d* Laura

*6 What was Phil Archer doing when he first noticed his
future wife Jill?*

  a Filming her with his ciné-camera at a church fête
  b Cleaning his tractor at Brookfield, covered in oil
  c Dressing up as a fortune teller at the summer fête
  d Collecting money for charity in Borchester

*7 Which member of the Archer family was born with a hole
in their heart?*

  a Shula   *b* Kenton
  c David   *d* Elizabeth

8 Where did David Archer study for 2 years?

  a Harper Adams College   *b* Royal Agricultural College
  c Ambridge Village Farmers Co-operative
  d Grange Farm School for Farmers

answers ➔ page 61

9 What is the name of Ruth and David's eldest child?

10 Who suffered from breast cancer in 2000?

11 What year did Grace Archer die in the stables fire?

12 Who is Jill Archer's sister-in-law?

13 From what position did Phil Archer retire?

- (a) Sea captain
- (b) Justice of the Peace
- (c) Bookie
- (d) Judo teacher

14 What was the name of Kenton Archer's one time business?

- (a) Archer's Antiquities
- (b) Kenton's café
- (c) Longbow Enterprises
- (d) Bodge it and Run

15 What was Dan Archer trying to do when he died of a heart attack?

- (a) Deliver a calf
- (b) Help a fallen sheep to stand up
- (c) Mend an old tractor for his grandson, John
- (d) Win a yard-of-ale contest at The Bull

16 What did David Archer abandon to witness the birth of his son, Joshua?

- (a) Meal at Grey Gables
- (b) Cricket match
- (c) Pint of shires
- (d) Tug of war competition

17 What does Jill Archer keep?

- (a) Goats
- (b) Rare old glass bottles
- (c) Bees
- (d) Roman coins

18 What did Jack (John) Archer become in 1953?

- (a) Lay preacher
- (b) Game keeper for the Berrow Estate
- (c) Reporter for the Borchester Echo
- (d) Landlord of The Bull

answers ➜ page 61

LA BELLE FRANCE!

Ambridge is twinned with a small town in France.
Can you remember the name of the town and how
the twinning affected some of the Ambridge residents?

1 What is the name of Ambridge's twin town?

a *St Emilion*   b *Bergerac*
c *Meyruelle*   d *Margaux*

2 Which region is the town situated in?

a *Languedoc-Roussillon, South of France*
b *Bordeaux*
c *Burgundy*
d *Alsace*

3 What was the name of the mayor who visited Ambridge?

a *Monsieur Robert Escargot*
b *Monsieur Gustave Touvier*
c *Monsieur Jean Aubert*
d *Monsieur Sid le Taureau*

**4 In 1993 a delegation from France visited Ambridge. Who
initiated this visit?**

a *Jill Archer*
b *Brian Aldridge*
c *Clarrie Grundy*
d *Marjorie Antrobus*

**5 What happened to Lynda Snell when the French delegation
was staying in Ambridge?**

a *She lost her voice*
b *She kept talking in Russian by mistake*
c *The mayor pinched her bottom*
d *She broke her leg*

answers ➜ page 62

6 Whose earthy charms did the French Mayor keep eyeing up?

a *Clarrie Grundy*
b *Julia Pargetter*
c *Ellen Rodgers*
d *Siobhan Hathaway*

7 In 1996 which singing duo won first prize in the Ambridge Talent Contest weekend for two in Meyruelle?

a *Ed and Fallon*
b *Lynda and Jill*
c *John and Hayley*
d *Eddie and Jolene*

8 What did Joe catch William doing while Clarrie and Eddie were away in Meyruelle?

a *Reading*
b *Smoking*
c *Poaching rabbits*
d *Watching 'Neighbours'*

CRYPTOGRAM

This description of *The Archers* has been encoded by replacing

each letter of the alphabet with another. We've started you off

with a letter (P=A) - can you work out the rest?

answers ➜ page 62

BUMBLE BEES

A lovely and familiar summer sound is the gentle humming of a passing bee. Did you know that there are several kinds of bees and can you name the ones below?

1 This bee is often out of hibernation in late February

a February bumble bee

b Early bumble bee

c First bumble bee

d Early to work bumble bee

2 This bee nests in grass and moss

a Grass bee

b Peacock bee

c Honey vole bee

d Moss carder bee

3 This bee can make a nest underground

a Mole bee

b Small earth bee

c Honey ant bee

d Treasure bumble bee

4 This bee shares its name with a bird

a Swift bee

b Mountain eagle bee

c Hill cuckoo bee

d Magpie bumble bee

5 This bee has a colour in its name

a Yellow and black bee

b Green, amber and red bee

c Orange legged bee

d Red-tailed bee

6 This is the biggest of our bees

a Buff-tailed bee

b Very big bee

c Blue-tailed bee

d Large legged bee

answers → page 62

HOLIDAY HOMEWORK

Can you help Daniel with his summer project? Many of us are
familiar with the common names of a variety of wildlife, but
Daniel needs to know their Latin names. This could be fun!

1 What is the field vole more formally known as?

a *Clethrionomys glassus*   b *Microtus agrestis*
c *Oakus volus*   d *Voleus fieldus*

2 What is a *Dama Dama*?

a *Blue deer*   b *Grey squirrel*
c *Fallow deer*   d *Wide-mouthed frog*

3 What is the *Vipera Berus*?

a *Common newt*   b *Adder*
c *Common frog*   d *Sand lizard*

4 What is a *Bombus Pratorum*?

a *Early bumble bee*   b *Late wasp*
c *Rowan tree*   d *Nettle (for nettle eating!)*

5 What is the wood violet called?

a *Viola sylvatica*   b *Geranium alba*
c *Viola quartet*   d *Nepeta viola*

6 What is the common daisy known as?

a *Commonus daisyus*
b *Bellis cucubalus*
c *Falco vipera*
d *Bellis perennis*

7 Which type of fly is the *Ephemeroptera*?

a *Junefly*   b *Aprilfly*
c *Septemberfly*   d *Mayfly*

answers ➜ page 62

TRUE OR FALSE

It's sometimes hard to separate truth from fiction. From the
statements listed below, can you tell which is true or false and
find out just how tight a grasp you have on reality . . . .

1 Phil Archer plays the organ.

2 Dick Pearson was the last landlord of the Cat & Fiddle.

3 The Grey Gables Country Club was built in the Tudor era.

4 Simon Gerrard was born in Canada.

5 Eddie Grundy has made a real record.

6 Wayne worked at Nelson's Wine Bar.

7 Gyp died in the fire at Grange Farm.

8 Doris Archer was Tom Forrest's sister.

9 Felpersham is a village.

10 Kathy Perks had an affair with PC Coverdale.

11 Siobhan Hathaway was born in Dublin.

*12 Neil Carter was a feed sales representative for
   Felpersham Mills.*

13 Ellen Rogers lives in Spain.

14 Sid Perks used to meet Jolene Rogers at the gym.

15 Usha Gupta bought Blossom Hill Cottage.

16 Jill Archer's maiden name was Greene.

17 Alf Grundy is a Justice of the Peace in Gloucestershire.

answers ➔ page 62

18 Fallon Rogers sang with Dross.

19 Susan Carter lives at No 2, The Green, Ambridge.

20 Underwoods in Borchester has a food hall.

MIXED UP KIDS!

The children of Ambridge have learned that growing up is hard to do! Can you help them to figure out who they really are? The letters in each segment of the circle, when combined with the mystery letter in the centre, form the names of six children who, despite being young, have led eventful lives . . . .

For more fun, name their lucky parents and guess the year in which each child was born!

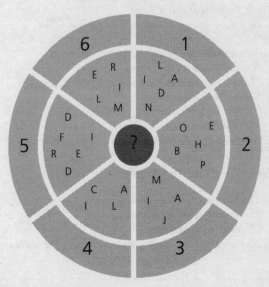

answers ➜ page 63

WHO ARE THEY?

From the clues given below, see how long it takes you
to identify these *Archers'* characters.

1 a *Her first three months were spent in a splint*
 b *By the age of 8 she was very keen on ponies*
 c *She rescued William Grundy, who was locked in an attic*
 d *In 2001 she started going out with a gamekeeper*

2 a *She was born in Germany*
 b *In 1978 she moved to Ambridge*
 c *She was an au pair at Home Farm*
 d *She married a policeman and moved to Plymouth*

3 a *At the age of 11 he was caught trespassing*
 b *When he was 17 he got his girlfriend pregnant*
 c *His daughter is called Kylie*
 d *He led an armed raid on the village Post Office*

4 a *At the tender age of five her parents divorced*
 b *Her father was named Roger*
 c *She was educated at Cheltenham Ladies College*
 d *She married a Canadian*

5 a *She came from Penny Hassett*
 b *She worked at the Village Shop*
 c *She lived in April Cottage*
 d *In 1972 she married a man called Joby*

6 a *This man was once an alcoholic*
 b *He has worked as a policeman*
 c *He comes from Yorkshire*
 d *He currently lives in the former Ambridge Police House*

answers ➔ page 64

RIDDLE ME REE

My first is in READING but not seen in BOOK

My second is in SOUND-BITE but not found in LOOK

My third is in MURMUR but never in BROOK

My fourth is in DISCORD but not seen in CHOIR

My fifth is not in DOLEFUL, you'll find it in DIRE

My sixth is in DRONING but not found in TUNE

My seventh is in BUZZING but not seen in CROON

My eighth is found in DRUMMING and also in THRUM

My whole is a tune that we all love to hum!

answers ➜ page 64

HOW DOES YOUR GARDEN GROW?

Martha Woodford was a country lass who loved flowers and knew their wonderful 'country' names. Can you pick out the seven country names for the summer flowers given below?

1 What is another name for 'Traveller's Joy'?

- *a* Traveller's rest
- *b* Old man's beard
- *c* Old man's stick
- *d* Penny hasset shrub

2 Which Ambridge cottage shares its name with a kind of honeysuckle?

- *a* Keeper's
- *b* Nightingale
- *c* Woodbine
- *d* April

3 What is 'Navelwort' also known as?

- *a* Sailorswort
- *b* Bellybutton wart
- *c* Twopence wort
- *d* Pennywort

4 Everyone knows this little cruciferous white flowered plant, but what's its common name?

- *a* Shepherd's crook
- *b* Shepherd's pocket
- *c* Shepherd's purse
- *d* Shepherd's shoe

5 'Hedge Convolvulus' is a familiar sight in country hedges. What is it more commonly known as?

- *a* Great hedge plant
- *b* Great bindweed
- *c* Little blighter
- *d* Little weed

6 You may have spotted the 'Ox-Eye' one summer in meadows or on a railway embankment. What is another, and prettier, name for it?

- *a* Moon daisy
- *b* Moon dandelion
- *c* Moon thistle
- *d* Moon weed

7 How else is the 'Lesser Hemlock' referred to?

- *a* Idiot's dill
- *b* Silly man's mustard
- *c* Fool's gold
- *d* Fool's parsley

answers ➔ page 64

EVENING ALL!

As Eddie knows, frittering away long summer evenings at
The Bull can get expensive! This bar tab contains 21 names.
Find ten matching couples taken from either column,
write down your answers in the table on the right, and you'll
discover the solitary drinker who hasn't paid their tab!

I.O.U	Jolene		I.O.U	
Dan	Peggy			
Caroline	David			
Martha	Mark			
Phil	Pru			
Brian	Siobhan			
Shula	Joby			
Tom	Jill			
Ruth	Guy			
Sid	Doris			
Jack	Jennifer			

answers ➜ page 64

BATS IN THE BELFRY

St Stephen's has its very own colony of bats but Bert Fry
is having difficulty identifying them for a conservation survey.
Can you help him?

1 This bat has rather large ears.

a *Short toed bat*

b *Carter gossip bat*

c *Common long-eared bat*

d *Large eared woolley bat*

2 This bat could do with a shave (like Bert!).

a *Hairy Borsetshire bat*

b *Whiskered bat*

c *Long bearded bat*

d *Blunt blade bat.*

**3 David and Ruth's daughter has something in common with
this bat.**

a *Little archer bat*

b *Farmers bat*

c *Tiny tawny bat*

d *Pipistrelle bat*

4 This bat may be seen late at night over a racecourse!

a *Lesser horseshoe bat*

b *Red Rum bat*

c *Greater bookie Bat*

d *Common favourite bat*

5 This bat is also known as the *Nyctalus leisleri*.

a *Lesser spotted Nyctalus*

b *Concord bat*

c *Leisler's bat*

d *Small lesley bat*

answers ➜ page 65

6 This bat gets up to no good at nights (like Eddie!)

a *Poaching bat*

b *Noctule bat*

c *Greater stayout bat*

d *Missing Bull cricket bat*

7 This bat sounds like it might have a lot to say.

a *Natterjack toad bat*

b *Natterer's bat*

c *Chatter bat*

d *Snoopy snell bat*

8 This bat is also known as the *Myotis doubentoni*.

a *Myotis mayfly*

b *Daylight robber*

c *Daubentons bat*

d *Ambridge gossip*

9 Which one of these is not a bat?

a *Noctule bat*

b *Bechsteins bat*

c *Common frog bat*

d *Pipistrelle bat*

10 Bats navigate by way of their sophisticated...?

a *Echo-locating system*

b *Eyesight*

c *Antennae*

d *Incredible sense of smell*

11 Don't worry, you won't find this bat in Ambridge. But what might *Desmodus rotundus* be?

a *Common mummy bat*

b *Common vampire bat*

c *Common frankenstein bat*

d *Common tucker bat*

answers → page 65

WORDSEARCH

ANIMALS OF AMBRIDGE

You've never heard them talk but can you see them?
Here are the clues to the names you'll find in the Wordsearch,
reading horizontally, vertically and diagonally. If you want to make it
easier you'll find the names upside-down at the foot of the page.
Spot the hidden word that unites them (4). Good luck!

Phil Archer's favourite pig (5)

William Grundy's turkey (the one he saved from being Christmas
Dinner!) (5)

The remaining peacock at The Bull (6)

The horse Grace Archer saved in 1955 (8)

One of Mrs Antrobus's favourite Afghan hounds (6)

Peggy Woolley's late cat (5)

Nelson's dog (7)

Dark bay gelding stolen from Caroline in 1993 (4)

Betty Tucker's favourite hen (6)

Eddie's ferret, one of a pair, named in memory of the spring flash
floods in Ambridge (4)

The Great Dane that accompanied Caroline Pemberton on her
arrival in Ambridge (3)

Dan Archer's old shire horse, one of a pair (5)

Lynda Snell's disappearing goat (7)

One of Dan's sheepdogs he trained after retirement (4)

Jack Woolley's Staffordshire Bull Terrier (7)

SOLUTIONS TO THE CLUES

Molly, Clint, Eccles, Midnight, Portia, Sammy, Charlie, Ippy, Ginger, Noah, Leo,
Boxer, Demeter, Nell, Captain

answers ➜ page 65

```
S G H M D N L E B G I N C A T I R P
I O N T Q A I S C D S E H L I N F O
P Y X C E L N T Y S A E R A P E T S
G S P L R D E H L L E M L E L D W I
M O N A A I M I G M D E H C R I H T
D I H R C H Y P I E O P A F C T R G
O C N T M O R L O A Y L I E S E I H
V E L G R P L M L R B E C L T X O N
N H O I B E D T E O S L D E A L M K
T E N I N G R H G X M N M O I T A E
E C H O X T Y W E Y I E N I P S C R
K C S P L A R C E P D M P R C L I E
M L F O Y S O L P D N O T O A W N X
Y I G R B M I C T H I D I C T O Q O
A N L T A S N R G K G T A N I R T B
L S G I N G E R D I H P N O M U S R
C O P A I Q I G Y G T X L E N I P A
R H E R T P M D E A B Y I N O P H M
E L A D E Y B P I R C H R H A P O A
P C B O G E O N T P M S A M M Y N I
D I M X N H L A I N E D T I V E C T
N S F G L C T H E R G N L B C H S R
```

answers ➜ page 65

AMBRIDGE FARMING FACTS

As you lean on a nearby stile chewing a piece of grass, take a moment
to ruminate over what you have learned about Ambridge farms...

*1 Where would you find 2 acres of Dutch cabbage
and 2 acres of leeks?*

- *a* Home Farm
- *b* The Village Shop
- *c* Lakey Hill
- *d* Bridge Farm

2 Where can you find Hereford Beef Cattle?

- *a* Brookfield Farm
- *b* Grange Farm
- *c* Grey Gables Country Park
- *d* Joe Grundy's lean to

3 What is the name of Brookfield Farm's sheepdog?

- *a* Gyp
- *b* Jet
- *c* Tess
- *d* Rover

4 What happened to the Grundy family in April 2000?

- *a* They found a very rare number plate.
- *b* Clarrie won a bathroom in a competition.
- *c* Brian Aldridge was kicked by a cow at Grange Farm.
- *d* They were evicted from Grange Farm.

5 Who is the local vet?

- *a* Tim Hathaway
- *b* Alistair Lloyd
- *c* Lawrence Lovell
- *d* Greg Turner

answers ➜ page 65

6 With what farming produce or activity would you associate Neil Carter and Betty Tucker?

a Free range eggs
b Bee keeping
c Yoghurt
d Hedge fencing

7 Who works at Pat's dairy?

a Betty Tucker
b Kirsty Miller
c Clarrie Grundy
d Fallon Rogers

8 With what place would you associate Fly the sheepdog?

a A wall
b Bridge Farm
c Grange Farm
d Home Farm

9 Who is the Chairman of Borchester Land?

a 'J.R.' Aldridge
b Matt Crawford
c Alfred Grundy
d Sir Sidney Goodman

10 In September 2002 who came to help out at Brookfield?

a Chaba
b Chappie
c Boris
d Snatch

11 Oliver Sterling is associated with what type of farming?

a Hobby farming
b Intensive farming
c Fish farming
d Beetroot farming

answers → page 66

HAPPY HOLIDAYS!

In the summer holidays Ruth and David took their three children on
a trip to the seaside. From the clues given below can you piece
together their itinerary, revealing the time of each activity,
who most enjoyed it and what they were wearing?

METHOD:

Use the grid opposite to record the information obtained by the clues
using a cross to mark a definite "no" and a tick to show a definite
"yes". Cross-reference your facts using a process of elimination until
all of the boxes are marked and the answers revealed.
Good luck logicians!

1 Josh couldn't wait to take his bucket and spade to the beach
as soon as the one wearing a green T-shirt finished their
favourite activity.

2 The one in the sunglasses loves swimming in the sea; this wasn't
David whose favourite activity came last.

3 Pip wore a sunhat to keep cool and her favourite activity
occurred in the afternoon. The puppet show began at 11am but
the two wearing hats were already bored by 11.15.

4 The family went on the Ferris wheel after Josh's chosen activity
but before that picked by the person sporting the purple T-shirt.

5 Ben wore the same style of top as the person who
loved ice-cream.

answers ➜ page 66

	David	Pip	Ben	Josh	Ruth	Green T-shirt	Purple T-shirt	Sunhat	Baseball cap	Sunglasses	Ferris wheel	Ice-cream parlour	Building sandcastles	Punch and Judy show	Swimming
9am															
11am															
1pm															
2pm															
4pm															
Ferris Wheel															
Ice-cream parlour															
Building sandcastles															
Punch and Judy show															
Swimming															
Green T-shirt															
Purple T-shirt															
Sunhat															
Baseball cap															
Sunglasses															

Time	Activity	Name	Attire

answers → page 66

"TIME GENTLEMEN PLEASE"

Sitting in a country pub garden watching the swallows fly by and finishing off a glass of Shires is a pleasant way to spend a balmy summer evening. While we're here let's have another drink and see how much we know about our very own Ambridge local.

1 Which of Sid Perks' wives was formerly called Mead?

2 Which former landlord had a drink problem?

3 Name Sid Perks' second wife.

4 Which family member did Sid lose in 1982?

5 What sort of sessions has Jolene run at The Bull?

a *Cookery classes*
b *Marriage guidance*
c *Line dancing*
d *Country and Western singing*

6 What was once known as The Playbar?

a *Coffee bar*
b *Room for dancing*
c *Smoking room*
d *Room for indoor cricket matches*

7 What was the theme of The Bull's restaurant when it served 'Olde English grubbe'?

a *Second World War*
b *American War of Independence*
c *War of the Roses*
d *English Civil War*

answers → page 66

8 Who did Bert Fry think that Owen 'the chef' was making advances to in The Bull in 1995?

a *Jill Archer*
b *Freda Fry*
c *Ruth Archer*
d *Caroline Pemberton*

9 Who was once a bar maid?

a *Pru Forrest*
b *Doris Archer*
c *Marjorie Antrobus*
d *Pip Archer*

10 When Kathy Perks asked Graham Ryder to value The Bull, what was his estimate?

a *£50,000*
b *£200,000*
c *£300,000*
d *£1,000,000*

11 In 1983 Julie the barmaid moved in with whom?

a *Neil Carter*
b *Sid Perks*
c *Brian Aldridge*
d *Nigel Pargetter*

12 What pub was run by Sid Perks' rival, Sean Myerson?

a *The Royal Oak*
b *The Crown*
c *The Cat & Fiddle*
d *The Snatch Arms*

13 What replaced the bowling green outside The Bull?

a *Bouncy castle*
b *Boule piste*
c *Statue of Jack Woolley*
d *Outdoor swimming pool*

answers ➜ page 66

14 Which century does The Bull date back to?

a *14th century*
b *15th century*
c *10th century*
d *20th century*

15 When does Sid serve 'stirrup cup'?

a *At a big darts match*
b *When Walter wanted one of his specials*
c *After a cricket match*
d *When the Hunt meets outside* The Bull

16 What is 'the little drummer boy'?

a *Ghost which haunts The Bull*
b *Painting by Walter Gabriel that hangs behind the bar*
c *Sid and Jolene's favourite song*
d *Name of a strong Borsetshire cider*

17 What is resident in The Bull garden?

a *Ferret*
b *Goat*
c *Peacock*
d *Eddie Grundy's old car*

18 Who is Sid Perks' step-daughter?

a *Lucy*
b *Kylie*
c *Fallon*
d *Kirsty*

19 What did Borchester Brewery insist that Peggy Archer do in 1953?

a *Take over the licence of The Bull*
b *Become a Borchester Brewery rep*
c *Stop doing Sunday lunches*
d *Stop serving spirits*

answers → page 66

SOLUTIONS

BROOKFIELD FARM AND THE ARCHER FAMILY

1   Dan Archer was born in 1896.

2   Doris Forrest was born in 1890 and married Dan Archer in 1921.

3   *a* Dan's younger brothers were called Frank and Ben.

4   *c* Phil Archer was born on St George's day (23 April 1928).

5   *c* George Fairbrother's only daughter was called Grace.

6   *a* Phil first noticed Jill when he filmed her with his ciné-camera at a church fête. The rest is history!

7   *d* Elizabeth Archer was born with a hole in her heart.

8   *b* David Archer studied at The Royal Agricultural College for two years.

9   David and Ruth's first child was named after her grandfather and is called Phillipa Rose (Pip for short).

10 Ruth Archer struggled with breast cancer in 2000 but seems to have made excellent recovery.

11 Grace Archer died in a stables fire at Grey Gables in 1955.

12 Christine Barford is Jill's sister-in-law.

13 *b* Phil Archer retired from acting as a Justice of the Peace.

14 *a* Kenton's one time business in Borchester was called Archer's Antiquities.

15 *b* Dan Archer died of a heart attack while helping a fallen sheep to stand up.

16 *b* David abandoned a cricket match to witness the birth of his son, Joshua.

17 *c* Jill keeps bees.

18 *d* Jack (John Archer) became landlord of The Bull in 1953.

15–18 Well done! You have modelled your life on Dan and Doris, are full of wisdom and are a pillar of the community.

10–15 Pretty good! You have modelled your life on Phil and Jill, meet setbacks with courage and probably have a daughter called Shula.

0–10 Could do better! You have modelled your life on David and Ruth, are incredibly busy and need to make time for The Archers (7.02 every evening except Saturdays, repeat at 2.00pm and Omnibus Sundays 10-11.15am. 92.7 Radio 4).

SUMMER

LA BELLE FRANCE!

1 c Ambridge is twinned with Meyruelle.
2 a Meyruelle is situated in the region of Languedoc-Roussillon.
3 b Monsieur Gustave Touvier was the mayor who visited Ambridge.
4 c Clarrie Grundy initiated the 1993 visit.
5 c The Mayor pinched Lynda's bottom. Ambridge is still reverberating with her response!
6 a The Mayor kept eyeing up Clarrie Grundy.
7 d Eddie and Jolene won first prize in the Ambridge Talent Contest, a weekend for two in Meyruelle. Jolene kindly gave her ticket to Clarrie so bloodshed was averted.
8 b Joe caught William smoking and was shocked as William was only thirteen.

| 1–2 correct Bon | 2–4 correct Meilleur | 4–6 correct Le mieux! |

CRYPTOGRAM

An everyday story of country folk

BUMBLE BEES

1 *b* Early bumble bee
2 *d* Moss carder bee
3 *b* Small earth bee
4 *c* Hill cuckoo bee
5 *d* Red-tailed bee
6 *a* Buff-tailed bee

HOLIDAY HOMEWORK

1 b The field vole is known as Microtus agrestis.
2 c A Dama dama is a fallow deer.
3 b The Vipera berus is an adder.
4 a The Bombus Pratorum is an early bumble bee
5 a The wood violet is called Viola sylvatica.
6 d The common daisy is known as Bellis perennis.
7 d The Ephemeroptera is the Mayfly.

TRUE OR FALSE

1 True. Phil Archer plays the organ.
2 False. Dick Pearson was the penultimate landlord of the Cat & Fiddle.
3 False. Grey Gables is Victorian mock Gothic, not Tudor!
4 True. Simon Gerrard was born in Canada.

SUMMER

5 True. Eddie Grundy has made a real record - with Jolene Rogers! (but unsurprisingly the company went bankrupt).

6 False. The name was Shane.

7 True. The Grundy family dog Gyp died in the fire at Grange Farm.

8 True. Doris Archer was Tom Forrest's sister.

9 False. Felpersham is a cathedral city.

10 False. Kathy didn't have an affair with PC Coverdale.

11 True. Siobhan Hathaway was born in Dublin.

12 False. Neil Carter was a feed sales representative for Borchester Mills.

13 True. Julia Pargetter's sister, Ellen Rogers, lives in Spain.

14 True. Sid Perks used to meet Jolene Rogers at the gym (and in the shower).

15 True. Usha Gupta bought Blossom Hill Cottage from Peggy Woolley in 1993.

16 False. Jill Archer's maiden name was Patterson.

17 False. Alf Grundy is Joe's eldest son and a petty thief.

18 True. Fallon Rogers sang with Dross.

19 False. The Carters live at No 1, The Green, Ambridge.

20 True. Underwoods has a food hall.

MIXED UP KIDS!

The mystery letter is 'E'

1 Shula's baby, Daniel, was conceived by IVF and born in 1994, nine months after his father, Mark Hebden, died in a car accident.

2 Kate Madikane (née Aldridge) gave birth to Phoebe in a teepee at the 1998 Glastonbury Festival. After Kate went to Africa Phoebe moved in with her father, Roy Tucker, and his wife, Hayley.

3 Jamie Perks was born just before the stroke of midnight on 20 July 1995. His parents separated in 1999 after Kathy discovered that Sid was having an affair with the tempting Jolene Rogers. Later they divorced.

4 Alice, Jennifer and Brian's youngest child, was born (in wedlock!) in 1988 and is now a feisty teenager.

5 Freddie was born only a few moments after his twin sister, Lily, soon before Christmas in 1999. While his parents, Elizabeth and Nigel Pargetter, pondered over what to call him he was known temporarily as 'Baby B'.

6 Kenton's estranged wife, Mel, gave birth to Meriel in Australia on 11May 2001. Due to the time difference, Jill heard about the birth of her sixth grandchild on 10 May; in effect before Meriel was even born!

WHO ARE THEY?

1 Helen Archer	2 Eva Coverdale (née Lenz)
3 Clive Horrobin	4 Debbie Gerrard (née Aldridge)
5 Martha Woodford	6 George Barford

> *Score. How many steps did you take before arriving at the correct solution?*
>
> *Mainly a* Congratulations. You not only listen once a week but a friend records the omnibus when you're away.
>
> *Mainly b* Excellent. You listen twice a week to make sure nothing changes!
>
> *Mainly c* Well done. You're a regular listener.
>
> *Mainly d* Not so good. Brush up on your background knowledge.
>
> *Mainly e* You need some help. Try reading 'Who's Who in The Archers!'

RIDDLE ME REE

The answer is Dum di dum

HOW DOES YOUR GARDEN GROW?

1 *b* Traveller's joy is another name for old man's beard.

2 *c* Honeysuckle is referred to as woodbine.

3 *d* Navelwort is also known as pennywort.

4 *c* Shepherd's purse.

5 *b* Great bindweed.

6 *a* Moon Daisy is a prettier name for the 'ox-eye'.

7 *d* 'Lesser hemlock' is often called fool's parsley.

All correct? Well done. Chances are you've been listening to *The Archers* since it first hit the airwaves in 1951!

EVENING ALL

Siobhan overlooked her tab!

BATS IN THE BELFRY

1	c	*The common long-eared bat*		2	b	*The whiskered bat*
3	d	*The pipistrelle bat*		4	a	*The lesser horseshoe bat*
5	c	*Leisler's bat*		6	b	*The noctule bat*
7	b	*The natterer's bat*		8	c	*Daubentons bat*
9	c	*Common frog bat*		10	a	*Echo-locating system*
11	b	*Common vampire bat*				

WORDSEARCH – PETS OF AMBRIDGE

The hidden word is PETS

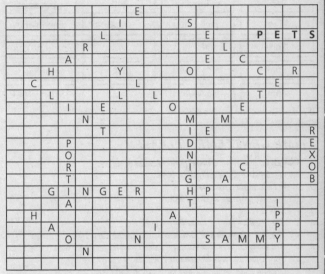

AMBRIDGE FARMING FACTS

1 *d* Leeks and cabbages are grown at Bridge Farm.

2 *a* Brookfield Farm farms Hereford Beef.

3 *b* Jet is Brookfield Farm's sheepdog.

4 *d* The Grundys were evicted from Grange Farm.

5 *b* Alistair Lloyd is the Ambridge vet.

SUMMER

6 *a*   Betty Tucker and Neil Carter produce free range eggs.

7 *c*   Clarrie Grundy works with Pat in the dairy.

8 *d*   Fly belongs to Home Farm.

9 *b*   Matt Crawford is Chairman of Borchester Land.

10 *a* Hungarian student, Chaba Progyani, helped out at Brookfield.

11 *a* Oliver Sterling is associated with Hobby farming.

HAPPY HOLIDAYS!

Time	Activity	Name	Attire
9am	swimming	Ruth	sunglasses
11am	punch & judy	Ben	green t-shirt
1pm	sandcastles	Josh	baseball cap
2pm	ferris wheel	Pip	sunhat
4pm	ice-cream	David	Purple t-shirt

If you persevered and got this one right you deserve the biggest Knickerbocker Glory going! Well done!

"TIME GENTLEMEN PLEASE!"

1   *Polly Perks, Sid's first wife, was formerly called Mead.*

2   *John (Jack) Archer had a drink problem.*

3   *Kathy Perks is Sid's second wife.*

4   *Sid lost Polly when she died in 1982.*

5 *c*   *Line dancing*

6 *a*   *The 'Playbar' was the name for the coffee bar.*

7 *d*   *The Bull restaurant was themed with the English Civil War.*

8 *b*   *Bert thought Owen was making advances towards his wife, Freda.*

9 *a*   *Pru Forrest was once barmaid at The Bull.*

10 *c* *Graham Ryder valued the pub for Kathy at £300,000.*

11 *a* *Julie the barmaid moved in with Neil Carter in 1983.*

12 *c* *Sean Myerson ran The Cat & Fiddle.*

13 *b* *A boule piste replaced the bowling green outside The Bull.*

14 *b* *The Bull dates back to the 15th century.*

15 *d* *Sid serves a 'stirrup cup' when the Hunt gathers outside The Bull.*

16 *a* *The ghost of 'a little drummer boy' is reputed to haunt The Bull.*

17 *c* *A peacock has taken up residence in The Bull garden.*

18 *c* *Fallon is Sid Perks' step-daughter.*

19 *a* *Borchester Brewery insisted that Peggy Archer take over the licence of The Bull in 1953.*

SUMMER

AUTUMN

AUTUMN BREAKS

Leaves are changing colour and falling from the trees,
and there's a snap in the air. It's time for an autumn break at the
Grey Gables Country Club. But how much do you know
about Ambridge's most famous hotel?

1 What sporting course lies beyond the gardens of Grey Gables?

*2 Name someone working at reception who is famous for her
village productions.*

3 Where does Jack Woolley come from?

- *a* Moseley, Birmingham
- *b* Stirchley, Birmingham
- *c* Ambridge, Borsetshire
- *d* Beirut, Lebanon

4 Peggy had nightmares of arriving at her wedding wearing what?

- *a* Suit of armour
- *b* Boy scout's uniform
- *c* Purple turban
- *d* Jockey's hat

5 What is Caroline Pemberton's job at Grey Gables?

- *a* Waitress
- *b* Administrator
- *c* Receptionist
- *d* Manager

*6 Gerald Grosvenor once appeared at Grey Gables. What is
his correct title?*

- *a* Lord Grosvenor
- *b* Squire of Penny Hassett
- *c* Duke of Westminster
- *d* Earl of Eton

7 Who was Assistant Manager at Grey Gables in 2002?

- *a* John Higgs
- *b* Roy Tucker
- *c* Lynda Snell
- *d* Trudy Porter

8 Who was Valerie Woolley?

- *a* Jack Woolley's sister
- *b* A cleaner at Grey Gables who was no relation to Jack
- *c* Jack Woolley's favourite dog
- *d* Jack Woolley's ex-wife

answers ➔ page 91

9 What is the name of Jack Woolley's step-daughter?

10 Grey Gables has a ballroom. True or false?

11 In what year did Jack and Peggy marry; 1990 or 1991?

12 What is Peggy's real first name?

13 What famous celebrity stayed at Grey Gables to play golf in 1989?

- *a* Noel Edmunds
- *b* Eric Sykes
- *c* Terry Wogan
- *d* Bob Monkhouse

14 What method of transport does Lynda Snell use to get to work?

- *a* Old butcher's bike
- *b* Motorised wheelbarrow
- *c* Aston Martin
- *d* Ford Capri

15 Who was Captain?

- *a* Head Chef
- *b* Jack's Staffordshire Bull Terrier
- *c* One of Peggy's nautical suitors, Godfrey Wendover
- *d* Head Gardener

16 What is the make of Jack's stylish car?

- *a* Jaguar
- *b* Mercedes
- *c* Bentley
- *d* Rolls Royce

17 For a short time Grey Gables' French chef, Jean-Paul, defected to where?

- *a* The Bull
- *b* Nelson's Wine Bar
- *c* The Dorchester
- *d* The Cat & Fiddle

18 What was the name of the rose that Jack Woolley specially commissioned for Peggy?

- *a* Ambridge Rose
- *b* Borsetshire Rose
- *c* Grey Gables Rose
- *d* Warm Woolley Rose

answers ➜ page 91

AMBRIDGE BIRD·LIFE

We all miss our summer visiting birds when they disappear in autumn. One bird in each group should have flown away by now. Which is it?

1 a *House sparrow*   b *Nuthatch*
   c *Swift*   d *Lapwing*

2 a *Robin*   b *Blue tit*
   c *Kingfisher*   d *Wryneck*

3 a *Green woodpecker*   b *Swallow*
   c *Little owl*   d *Magpie*

4 a *Corn bunting*   b *Jay*
   c *Sedge warbler*   d *Collared dove*

5 a *Jackdaw*   b *Willow tit*
   c *Cuckoo*   d *Long-tailed tit*

6 a *Yellowhammer*   b *Lesser spotted woodpecker*
   c *Bullfinch*   d *House martin*

7 a *Hobby*   b *Buzzard*
   c *Sparrowhawk*   d *Kestrel*

8 a *Barn owl*   b *Goldcrest*
   c *Willow warbler*   d *Blackbird*

9 a *Sandmartin*   b *Robin*
   c *Great tit*   d *Tawny owl*

10 a *Long-eared owl*   b *Nightingale*
    c *Jackdaw*   d *Rook*

answers ➜ page 92

THE ARCHERS
& OTHER ANIMALS

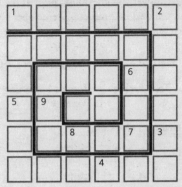

Can you put the words into the spiral helped by the clues?
The last letter of each word is the first letter of the next, and they
begin outside and spiral clockwise into the centre

1 Archer black sheep

2 Looks good in a gorilla suit

3 Nice with mint sauce

4 Local radio star reporter

5 Good with animals

6 Brian Aldridge behaved like one

7 Sausage entrepreneur

8 Cows say it

9 Caroline's amore

answers ➜ page 92

THE AMBRIDGE SHOOT

Test your general knowledge of The Archers with this quick fire round. The first answer you give must count as the final one and you must finish the quiz in 2 minutes! Remember – you have only one shot at each question! Get ready – finger on the trigger – GO!

1 What is the name of Mike and Betty Tucker's son?

2 Name one of Tom Archer's girlfriends beginning with K and ending in Y.

3 Who is Joe Grundy's elder son?

4 Who is Jennifer Aldridge's sister?

5 Which member of the Archer family comes from Prudhoe?

6 Name the last receptionist for Dr Hathaway's practice

7 What is the maiden name of Sid Perks's third wife?

8 Who did Debbie Aldridge marry?

9 Who lives in the Old Police House?

10 Which farm in Ambridge was the first to go organic?

11 What do St George and Phil Archer have in common?

12 Who are Phoebe Aldridge's natural parents?

13 Who is Tony Archer's mother?

14 What is Lawrence Lovell generally called?

15 Who is the manager of Grey Gables?

16 What was the name of Shula's first husband?

answers ➔ page 92

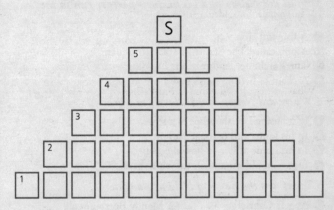

17 Who bought Grange Farm in 2000?

18 What was Susan Carter's maiden name?

19 What was Doris Archer's maiden name?

20 What did Jethro Larkin call Phil Archer?

ARCHERS PYRAGRAM

Solve the anagrams to find out the word running down the middle of the pyramid

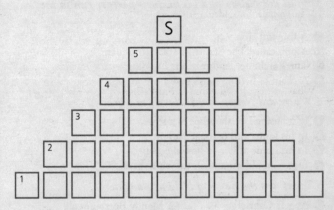

S

5

4

3

2

1

5 EON

4 FLESH

3 A SMILER

2 LEVER SELL

1 SEES LESS SUN

answers → page 91

ARMCHAIR MEMORIES
– NELSON GABRIEL

Nelson Gabriel has been much missed in Ambridge. His quick wits and sardonic comments hid a warm heart and he was a loyal friend. How much can you remember of his long life and chequered career?

1 Which of the forces did Nelson join for his National Service?

2 Who did Nelson persuade to lend him £3000 to invest in an engineering business in 1961?

3 What did Nelson and his business partner run in the early 1960s?

ⓐ A fish and chip van
ⓑ A pub called The Statue in Trafalgar Square
ⓒ The Borchester cricket team
ⓓ A chain of betting shops and a casino

4 Where did Nelson want Clarrie to work?

ⓐ In a business rival's office as a spy
ⓑ In his sauna and massage parlour
ⓒ In his home as live-in housekeeper
ⓓ Down an old mine shaft in Felpersham.

5 What was the name of Nelson's daughter?

ⓐ Angela Gabriel   ⓑ Mandy Beesborough
ⓒ Rosemary Tarrant   ⓓ Trina Muir

6 What did Nelson and Julia Pargetter do in the ballroom one New Year's Eve?

ⓐ Kissed
ⓑ Played cards
ⓒ Decided to elope to Gretna Green
ⓓ Had a fencing duel

answers ➜ page 93

7 Where is Nelson buried?
a Spain
b Argentina
c Ambridge
d Brazil

IF YOU GO DOWN TO THE WOODS TODAY!

There's nothing nicer than rambling in the countryside gathering wild berries. See if you can pick out the berries from their clever impersonators in the choices below.
(Remember some berries have to be cooked before they are eaten, while others can be very poisonous – so if in doubt don't pick them or ask Bert Fry first!)

Which are berries?

1   a   Snowberry   b   Sowberry
    c   Sourberry   d   Sunberry

2   a   Sheepberry   b   Pigberry
    c   Cowberry   d   Horseberry

3   a   Crampberry   b   Cranberry
    c   Crankberry   d   Crumberry

4   a   Nasty bramble   b   Sharp bramble
    c   Itchy bramble   d   Stone bramble

5   a   Raspberry   b   Waspberry
    c   Beeberry   d   Banberry

6   a   Joeberry   b   Bertberry
    c   Bilberry   d   Daveberry

answers → page 93

WORDSEARCH

THINGS THAT GO BUMP IN THE NIGHT!

It's Hallowe'en and there are all manner of scary things in our
wordsearch. Here are the clues to the ghoulish words you'll find
reading vertically, horizontally, diagonally and backwards.
If you want to make it easier we've put the names upside-down
at the foot of the page, and there's one extra hidden word
which links these answers (9). Good luck!

Some say that Lynda rides one (10)

Tom Forrest found these in St Stephen's (4)

Legendary ghost dog (8)

Ghost that haunts The Bull (7, 3)

Kenton's Hallowe'en costume in 2002 (7)

Unlucky number (8)

The vegetable used to make Jack-o'-lanterns (7)

A cunning Grundy plan to make money (9)

It wriggled and jiggled and tickled inside her (6)

First name of the April Cottage ghost (7)

Some think that Lynda is one (5)

Girls might need this to woo Tom (6)

Brian Aldridge has several of these in his closet (9)

```
B L O H D S P T W Q F E M R D X P F
F P S G O R N R A R K M R R B R L I
B I H P B D C O S H N C U S O O T D
G A B O I A L I T N P M B T R N W H
R Q N T K D T C S E T A K R M C O A
E D A S F S E U B E L Z I H A U F L
E N U L Y M U R G T N E R T B C N L
N U R A C I O N D R A M K W A L B O
T O E D H P H M D I D C L S O H U W
I H X M R T U M P H I U A B H O T E
W B O P U U I S A T B O H F S G P E
C O F L R K M R S R Q P M W P H N N
I H R E B U D M N F C P O T I O N U
T K B P M I O I E D X G O H E S R L
O S P A K O P T P R E R B I N T O D
L P I U R W S K H K B P S T B W U E
W M K B M A T C I R S O K N M A D H
O D R A C U L A S N E U Y I U L N C
P O D T Q D O C B O R N Z T P K S T
N T E S N H L K H D E C M S S E L I
B A O B G S P U M P K I N A T A O W
L H A K R D C S N I O W P B L E K S
```

answers ➜ page 94

ODD ONE OUT

Ambridge is a small community, and over the years
a lot of links have been forged among its inhabitants. Can you
identify the odd one out in the following groups?

1 Who has not had a romantic liaison with Caroline Bone?

a Robin Stokes   *b* Brian Aldridge
c Nigel Pargetter

2 Who does not work at Bridge Farm?

a Colin Kennedy   *b* Tom Archer
c Alf Grundy

3 Who has not been a practising solicitor?

a Usha Gupta   *b* Matthew Thorogood
c Mark Hebden

4 Who has not been a Church Warden at St. Stephen's?

a Bert Fry   *b* Shula Hebden Lloyd
c Kate Madikane

5 Who is not one of Phil Archer's grandchildren?

a Meriel   *b* Phoebe
c Lily

6 Who is not one of William Grundy's godparents?

a Caroline Pemberton   *b* Sid Perks
c Jack Woolley

7 Who has not been barred from The Bull?

a Jazzer   *b* Janet Fisher
c Eddie Grundy

8 Who refused to go on the 2002 Countryside March in London?

a Oliver Sterling   *b* Jennifer Aldridge
c Jill Archer

answers ➔ page 94

RIDDLE ME REE

My first is in ANCIENT but isn't in OLD

My second is in LEGEND but never in TOLD

My third is in TREASURE and also in CHEST

My fourth is in RIGHTEOUS though never in BLESSED

My fifth is not in SUNSHINE, you'll see it in MOON

My sixth is not in FAVOUR, you'll find it in BOON

My seventh is in SUPPER but isn't in MEAL

My eighth is in FICTITIOUS and not seen in REAL

My whole is a lady who has great appeal

answers ➜ page 94

LIFE WITH THE TUCKERS

Autumn can be a lovely season in the country, even for milkmen making early deliveries. See how much you know about Ambridge's famous moaning milkman, Mike Tucker, his long-suffering wife and his family

1 What is Betty's day job?

a *Receptionist at* Grey Gables

b *Barmaid at* The Bull

c *Assistant at the village shop*

d *Traffic warden*

2 What was Hayley Tucker's maiden name?

a *Tarrant*

b *Jordan*

c *Gordon*

d *Horrobin*

3 Who left Neil Carter a patch of land at Willow Farm in 1986?

a *Mike Tucker*

b *Bill Insley*

c *Jack Woolley*

d *Brian Aldridge*

4 What local union branch did Mike set about reviving?

a *NUAAW*

b *NUT*

c *Unison*

d *RAC*

5 Where did Roy Tucker and Hayley first set up home together?

a *Grange Farm*

b *Royal Suite at Grey Gables*

c The Bull

d *Nightingale Farm*

6 Lilian Bellamy's 'toy boy' was beloved by Brenda. What was his first name?

a *Simon*

b *Cameron*

c *Scott*

d *Leon*

7 In 1998 Roy Tucker was dumbfounded when Hayley told him what?

a *She worked for MI5*

b *Kate Aldridge was pregnant*

c *Joe Grundy had been awarded a knighthood*

d *Willow Farm had been burnt down*

8 What was the name of Betty's farm shop at Ambridge Farm?

a *Betty's Barn*

b *Tucker's Goodies*

c *Free Range Betty*

d *Tucker Enterprizes*

9 Who was Mike Tucker's partner for 'Pick your own strawberries'?

a *William Grundy*

b *Eddie Grundy*

c *Greg Turner*

d *Neil Carter*

10 What part of Mike's body was injured when he was hit by an hydraulic pipe?

a *Eye*

b *Leg*

c *Arm*

d *Foot*

answers ➜ page 95

ST STEPHEN'S CHURCH

At Harvest Festival local produce is piled high in St Stephen's
Church. How plentiful is your ecclesiastical knowledge?
Find out here!

1 St Stephen's was built on the site of an early 7th Century
Augustinian church. When was it consecrated?

- *a* 1177
- *b* 1281
- *c* 1066
- *d* 1700

2 In 1990 the clock weights crashed through the floor,
narrowly missing whom?

- *a* The Bishop of Felpersham
- *b* Bert Fry
- *c* William Grundy
- *d* Roy Tucker

3 Who, or what, took up residence in the church at
St Stephen's in June 1976?

- *a* Cat called Walter
- *b* Red kites
- *c* Grundys fleeing from persecution
- *d* Colony of flittermice bats

4 Which of these is a part of a church?

- *a* King
- *b* Queen
- *c* Nave
- *d* Ace

answers ➔ page 95

5 What might you call the principal church of a Diocese?

a High Church

b Cathedral

c Royal Monastery

d Steeple Church

6 What is an underground chamber called in a church?

a Crypt

b Tomb Room

c Apse

d Buttress

7 In 1959 a memorial window was installed. Who was this to commemorate?

a Ralph Bellamy

b Grace Archer

c Dan Archer

d John Wooldridge, the late Bishop of Felpersham

8 What did Dan Archer find near the church bells in 1976?

a Hoard of civil war coins

b Swarm of bees

c Nest of red kites

d Badger

9 Who was a former vicar at St Stephen's?

a Robin Loxley

b Robin Macy

c Robin Fisher

d Robin Stokes

10 Where did Janet Fisher go on the Jubilee 2000 Third World debt march?

a Paris

b Cologne

c Madrid

d Berlin

answers ➜ page 95

COUNTRY NAMES
FOR COUNTRY PLACES

Over time and in different places the meanings of words can
change. See if you can identify the correct meanings of old terms
from the choices below:

1 What is a barrow?

a   *Wheelbarrow without a wheel*
b   *County*
c   *Ancient burial mound*
d   *Roman spa town*

2 What is a beck?

a   *River*
b   *Hill*
c   *Beer*
d   *Forest*

3 What is another old name for an enclosed space?

a   *Mere*
b   *Garth*
c   *Thorpe*
d   *Ard*

4 What is a ford?

a   *Old car*
b   *Wood at the top of a hill*
c   *Valley*
d   *River crossing*

5 What is a don?

a   *Home for an Oxford tutor*
b   *Hill fort*
c   *Monastery*
d   *Wood*

answers ➜ page 95

6 What is the old word for a market?

a *Stable*
b *Table*
c *Able*
d *Cable*

7 If a place name ended with 'holt' where might you expect it to be?

a *On a hill*
b *By a lake*
c *In a wood*
d *In a valley*

8 What does the 'Hart' represent on a pub sign (as in The White Hart)?

a *Dog*
b *Stag*
c *Shield*
d *Cart*

9 What does 'by' mean at the end of a place name?

a *Walled Roman town*
b *Church or pub*
c *Farm or village*
d *River or lake*

10 What is a 'hoe' when related to a place name (as in Plymouth Hoe)?

a *Place with an agricultural museum*
b *Spur or ridge*
c *Pile of stones*
d *Lock*

11 What does Chipping usually mean (as in Chipping Sodbury).

a *Village of carpenters*
b *Cave dwellers*
c *Town with an abbey*
d *Market or market place*

answers ➔ page 95

FAIR GAME

The Aldridge shoots are renowned throughout the county of Borsetshire (as are Jennifer's hampers). Are you a Greg Turner, a George Barford or a William Grundy? See how much you know about our British Game and find out!

1 Which is not a game bird?

- *a* Wood Pigeon
- *b* Red Grouse
- *c* Red Kite
- *d* Partridge

2 Name the game bird from the choices below.

- *a* Partridge
- *b* Kingfisher
- *c* Borsetshire Beauty
- *d* Moorhen

3 What game animal does Brian Aldridge farm?

- *a* Wild boar
- *b* Snails
- *c* Goat
- *d* Deer

4 What is a traditional game dish?

- *a* Caramelised carrot
- *b* Jugged hare
- *c* Toad-in-the-hole
- *d* Roast gooseberry

5 What do Eddie Grundy's ferrets like to hunt?

- *a* Pheasants
- *b* Rabbits
- *c* Quail
- *d* Darts

answers → page 91

6 *What kind of meat is venison?*

a Sheep
b Deer
c Boar
d Goat

7 *What is a mallard?*

a Duck
b Pigeon
c Quail
d Partridge

8 *What is traditionally shot on the 'Glorious 12th'?*

a Pumpkins
b Terrine
c Hare
d Grouse

JOE'S LIST

Autumn finds Joe Grundy in front of the fire in The Bull scamming as many pints of Shires as he can.

Unscramble the letters to reveal the six things Joe Grundy would least like to find in the pub.

1 SELAITWLH
2 UDINEGEYDDR
3 MERBAREW
4 RABYBLET
5 AOWMGDOAON!
6 ZPEHUIQTBU

answers → page 96

THE ARCHERS OF BRIDGE FARM

Pat and Tony Archer have lived at Bridge Farm since 1978 and a lot of water has passed under the bridge since then! Find out whether you're a friend, relative, clone or stranger.

1 What terrible event took place on Tom Archer's 17th birthday?

a *Dan Archer died*
b *Tom's brother John was killed in a tractor accident*
c *Pat was involved in a car accident*
d *Tony fell through Bridge Farm roof*

2 What is the name of Tony Archer's mother?

a *Peggy Woolley*
b *Doris Archer*
c *Laura Archer*
d *Mary Pound*

3 What borders Bridge Farm?

a *Lakey Hill*
b *Heydon Berrow*
c *An army camp*
d *Grey Gables*

4 What is the name of Pat and Tony's shop in Borchester?

a *Take a Leek*
b *Organic Farm Shop*
c *Ambridge Organics*
d *Helen's Hideaway*

5 What did Pat Archer captain in her early days in Ambridge?

a *Ladies' football team*
b *River Am steam boat*
c *Cat & Fiddle darts team*
d *Ambridge Scrabble Team*

answers → page 96

6 Where did John Archer meet Hayley Jordan?

a *Hollerton Junction*

b *In a strawberry field*

c *Borchester Young Farmers' Christmas bash*

d *Club in Birmingham*

7 Tom Archer was charged with criminal damage. What for?

a *Joy riding and crashing a car*

b *Destroying part of a genetically modified rape crop*

c *Smashing windows in the village hall*

d *Pushing George Barford into the River Am*

8 With whom did Helen Archer form a romantic liaison in the summer of 2001?

a *Oliver Sterling*

b *Eddie Grundy*

c *Greg Turner*

d *Simon Gerrard*

9 What did Tom Archer want to name 'Ambridge Originals'?

a *His band*

b *Helen's cheeses*

c *His parents*

d *His pork sausages*

10 Where did Pat Archer wish to take her children in 1984?

a *On a world cruise*

b *To Disneyland*

c *On a CND march*

d *Mountaineering in Wales*

11 What did Hayley do when John Archer asked her to marry him?

a *Faint*

b *Say no*

c *Tell him she was already married*

d *Say yes*

answers → page 96

12 Who works for Pat in the Bridge Farm dairy?

a *Betty Tucker*

b *Mrs Pullen*

c *Ed Grundy*

d *Clarrie Grundy*

13 What did Tony and Pat ask Helen to do on her 21st birthday?

a *Go easy on the Grange Farm apple brandy*

b *Try and be nice to everyone, just once*

c *Stop annoying her younger brother*

d *Run their new shop in Borchester*

14 What relation is Phil Archer to Tony?

a *Cousin*

b *Uncle*

c *Brother-in-law*

d *Step-brother*

15 What relation is Christine Barford to Tony?

a *Sister*

b *Sister-in-law*

c *Aunt*

d *Cousin*

16 Name the girls two-timing Tom double-dated Christmas 2000

a *Lauren and Fallon*

b *Kate and Kirsty*

c *Kirsty and Lauren*

d *Thelma and Louise*

answers ➜ page 96

SOLUTIONS

AUTUMN BREAKS

1   The Golf Course lies beyond the gardens of Grey Gables.

2   Lynda Snell is a receptionist.

3   *b* Jack Woolley comes from Stirchley, Birmingham.

4   *c* Peggy was afraid she would turn up at her wedding wearing a purple turban.

5   *d* Caroline Pemberton is Manager.

6   *c* Gerald Grosvenor's correct title is the Duke of Westminster.

7   *d* Trudy Porter was Assistant Manager in 2002.

8   *d* Valerie Woolley was Jack Woolley's ex-wife. The marriage was unhappy and the couple separated in 1968, and finally divorced in 1974.

9   Hazel was the daughter of Reggie and Valerie Trentham who ran Grey Gables in the 1950s. Valerie married Jack Woolley after Reggie died.

10   True. Grey Gables has a ballroom.

11   Jack and Peggy married in 1991.

12   Peggy's first name is Margaret.

13   *c* Terry Wogan booked into the Royal Garden Suite to play golf in 1989. Not only did listeners hear his mellifluous tones but also the rarely heard voice of Pru Forrest, played by Judi Dench, as she presented him with a pot of damson jam.

14   *a* Lynda is often seen on an old butcher's bike (not to be confused with her being the village bike – that privilege was once Caroline Pemberton's although Siobhan Hathaway and Brenda Tucker are hot contenders).

15   *b* Captain was Jack's much loved Staffordshire Bull Terrier.

16   *c* Jack's car is a Bentley.

17   *b* Jean-Paul defected to Nelson's Wine Bar.

18   *a* The rose commissioned from David Austin by Jack is called The Ambridge Rose.

15–18 correct Gold medal! No-one can teach you anything about The Archers. You have clearly listened all your life

10–15 correct. Silver medal! You probably started listening in the seventies but will soon make up lost ground.

5–10 correct. Bronze medal! You're a new listener. Well done for a gallant attempt.

AMBRIDGE BIRD LIFE

These are the birds who stayed in Ambridge when they should have flown off to a warmer climate:

1	c	Swift	2	d	Wryneck
3	b	Swallow	4	c	Sedge warbler
5	c	Cuckoo	6	d	House martin
7	a	Hobby	8	c	Willow warbler
9	a	Sandmartin	10	b	Nightingale

ARCHERS & OTHER ANIMALS

THE AMBRIDGE SHOOT QUICK FIRE ROUND

See how well you've done!

1   Roy Tucker is the Tuckers' son.
2   Kirsty Miller is the name of Tom's girlfriend.
3   Alfred Grundy is Joe Grundy's elder son.
4   Lilian Bellamy is Jennifer Aldridge's sister.
5   Ruth Archer comes from Prudhoe.
6   Susan Carter was the last receptionist for Dr Hathaway's practice.
7   Jolene Rogers is Jolene Perks' maiden name.
8   Debbie Aldridge married Simon Gerrard.
9   Christine and George Barford live at the Old Police House.
10 Bridge Farm was the first farm in Ambridge to go organic.
11 April 23rd is both Phil's birthday and St George's Day.
12 Roy Tucker and Kate Aldridge (now Madikane) are Phoebe Tucker's natural parents.
13 Peggy Woolley is Tony Archer's mother.
14 Lawrence Lovell is generally known as Larry.
15 Caroline Pemberton manages Grey Gables.
16 Mark Hebden is the name of Shula Hebden Lloyd's first husband.
17 Oliver Sterling bought Grange Farm in 2000.

18 *Susan Horrobin is Susan Carter's maiden name.*
19 *Doris Forrest is Doris Archer's maiden name.*
20 *Jethro Larkin called Phil Archer 'Boss.'*

> **20 correct.** *Congratulations – you are Felpersham's Finest! A game hamper and two bottles of vintage ruby port for you.*
>
> **15–20 correct.** *Excellent. Two brace of pheasants and a bottle of cognac for you.*
>
> **10–15 correct.** *Not bad at all. One brace of pheasants and a bottle of Famous Grouse for you.*
>
> **0–5 correct.** *Oh dear! A wood pigeon and a bottle of mineral water for you - to help steady your aim!*

ARCHERS PYRAGRAM

ARMCHAIR MEMORIES – NELSON GABRIEL

1   Nelson joined the RAF but managed never to fly!

2   Nelson's father, Walter Gabriel, made his son the first of many loans in 1961.

3   *d*   Nelson and Walter ran a chain of betting shops and a casino in the sixties.

4   *b*   Nelson wanted Clarrie Grundy to work in his sauna and massage parlour.

5   *c*   Nelson's daughter is called Rosemary Tarrant.

6   *a*   Nelson and Julia Pargetter shared a kiss.

7   *c*   Nelson is buried at St Stephen's Church, Ambridge.

IF YOU GO DOWN TO THE WOODS TODAY

1	a	Snowberry	2 c	Cowberry
3	b	Cranberry	4 d	Stone bramble
5	a	Raspberry	6 c	Bilberry

AUTUMN

WORDSEARCH
– THINGS THAT GO BUMP IN THE NIGHT

The hidden word is HALLOWEEN

				S											F
	S				N									L	
		P				O							O		
			I				T	N				R			H
	D			D				E			R				A
	D			E			E	E	L		I				L
	N				R			T		E					L
	U					R		R			K				O
	O	D						I		C	S				W
	H		R					H	I						E
	B			U				T					G		E
	O				M		S						H		N
	H				M				P	O	T	I	O	N	
				O		E							S		
			O				R						T		
		R						B					W		
		B							O				A		H
D	R	A	C	U	L	A				Y			L		C
		T											K		T
		S													I
				P	U	M	P	K	I	N					W

ODD ONE OUT

1	*c* Nigel Pargetter	2	*c* Alf Grundy
3	*b* Matthew Thorogood	4	*c* Kate Madikane
5	*b* Phoebe	6	*c* Jack Woolley
7	*b* Janet Fisher	8	*c* Jill Archer

RIDDLE ME REE

The answer is Antrobus

LIFE WITH THE TUCKERS

1 c *Betty works at the Village Shop.*
2 b *Hayley's maiden name is Jordan.*
3 b *Bill Insley died in 1986 leaving Neil Carter a patch of land around the house at Willow Farm.*
4 a *Mike revived the NUAAW. Extra points if you know what the abbreviation stands for! (National Union of Agricultural and Allied Workers).*
5 d *Roy and Hayley Tucker first set up home as tenants of Mrs Antrobus at Nightingale Farm.*
6 c *Scott Daniels captured Brenda's heart but let her down, just as he did Lilian.*
7 b *Hayley told Roy that Kate Aldridge was pregnant. Roy knew there was a distinct possibility that he was the father!*
8 a *Betty's farm shop at Ambridge Farm was called Betty's Barn.*
9 d *Neil Carter was Mike Tucker's partner for 'Pick your own strawberries'.*
10 a *The hydraulic pipe hit Mike in the eye.*

ST STEPHEN'S CHURCH

1 **b** St Stephen's was consecrated in 1281.
2 **c** The clock weights narrowly missed William Grundy.
3 **d** A colony of bats - flittermice - took up residence in the Church.
4 **c** The nave is the main space of a church.
5 **b** The principal church of a diocese is called a Cathedral.
6 **a** An underground chamber is called a crypt.
7 **b** A memorial window was installed to commemorate Grace Archer.
8 **b** Dan Archer and Betty Tucker found a swarm of bees near one of the church bells in 1976.
9 **d** Robin Stokes was a former vicar of St Stephen's.
10 **b** Janet Fisher and Usha Gupta went to Cologne on the Jubilee 2000 Third World debt march.

5–10 answers correct? You are a pillar of your community and worthy of respect!

4–1 answers correct? You must go to church more often!

COUNTRY NAMES FOR COUNTRY PLACES

1 c *Ancient burial mound*
2 a *River*
3 b *Garth*
4 d *River crossing*
5 b *Hill fort*
6 a *Stable*
7 c *Wood*
8 b *Stag*
9 c *Farm or village*
10 b *Spur or ridge*
11 d *Market or market place*

FAIR GAME

1	*c* Red kite	2	*a* Partridge
3	*d* Deer	4	*b* Jugged hare
5	*b* Rabbits	6	*b* Deer
7	*a* Duck	8	*d* Grouse

JOE'S LIST

1	SELAITWLH	HIS WALLET
2	UDINEGEYDDR	EDDIE GRUNDY
3	MERBAREW	WARM BEER
4	RABYBLET	BARTLEBY
5	AOWMGDOAON!	A GOOD WOMAN!
6	ZPEHUIQTBU	THE PUB QUIZ

THE ARCHERS OF BRIDGE FARM

1 *b* Tom's brother John was killed in a tractor accident.

2 *a* Peggy Woolley is Tony's mother.

3 *b* Heydon Berrow borders Bridge Farm.

4 *c* Ambridge Organics is the name of Pat and Tony's shop in Borchester.

5 *a* Pat captained a ladies' football team.

6 *d* John Archer met Hayley Jordan at a club in Birmingham.

7 *b* Tom destroyed part of a genetically modified rape crop.

8 *c* Helen became romantically linked with gamekeeper Greg Turner.

9 *d* Tom wanted to call his pork sausages 'Ambridge Originals'.

10 *c* Typically, Pat wanted to take her children on a CND march.

11 *b* Hayley said no to John Archer's proposal of marriage.

12 *d* Clarrie Grundy works for Pat in the dairy.

13 *d* Pat and Tony asked Helen to run their new shop Ambridge Organics on her 21st birthday.

14 *b* Phil Archer is Tony's uncle.

15 *c* Christine Barford is Tony's aunt.

16 *c* Tom two-timed Kirsty and Lauren.

---

16 correct. You want to know all about Pat and Tony, and what you don't know you make up!

12–16 correct. You are surprised at how much you know about Pat and Tony and would like to know them better.

6–12 correct. You take a friendly interest in Bridge Farm but have a lot on your mind.

0–6 correct. You're far too busy to be bothered with Pat and Tony and have better things to do.

WINTER

SEASONS GREETINGS

There's nothing better on a cold winter's day than settling by the
fire with pen, paper and *The Archers Quiz Book* by your side!
Here are some teasers to get you in the mood.

1 What did we hear Dan first say on 1 January 1951?

a Sorry I'm late Doris but even on New Year's Day the cows
have to be milked

b Here's a toast to the future. Let's hope for many more happy
years in Ambridge

c And a Happy New Year to all

d Put on the radiogram, Phil, there's a new radio serial I want to
listen to

2 What musical instrument did Walter Gabriel play at the annual Christmas Carol Service?

a Didgeridoo

b Euphonium

c Sitar

d Mandolin

3 Which Ambridge couple got married on a Christmas Day?

a Sid Perks and Kathy Holland

b Alistair Lloyd and Shula Hebden

c Jennifer Archer and Roger Travers-Macy

d Joby Woodford and Martha Lily

4 Which Ambridge couple got married on New Year's Day?

a Duncan Gemmell and Lucy Perks

b Jack Woolley and Peggy Archer

c Nigel Pargetter and Elizabeth Archer

d Eddie Grundy and Clarrie Larkin

answers ➜ page 122

GOOD FOOD HEARTY CHEER

Good food and hearty cheer certainly help us get through
the winter months and we all have our favourite treats.
See if you can work out what connections certain
Ambridge folk have with food and drink.

1 In what food product did John Archer specialize?

a *He created Bridge Farm freshly pulled leek soup*

b *He held the Borsetshire record for baked bean eating*

c *He produced organic pork*

d *He introduced kangaroo farming to Ambridge*

2 Brian Aldridge once got very drunk at Grange Farm – on what?

a *Clarrie's Xmas trifle*

b *Joe's home made apple brandy schnapps*

c *Eddie's Coq au vin*

d *Calvados Eddie brought back from France*

3 Who is the gastronomic genius of Grey Gables?

a *Jean Floyd*   b *Fat Paul*

c *Jean-Paul*   d *Jacques Aubert*

4 What's the favourite beer at The Bull?

a *Anymores (as in "any more for any more?")*

b *Coming Up Special Best*

c *Archers*

d *Shires*

5 What did Joe Grundy put in his home brewed cider?

a *Pair of overalls (to give it more colour)*

b *Lump of meat*

c *Pair of socks*

d *Bert Fry's prize-winning cabbage*

answers → page 122

RIDDLE ME REE

My first is in MINCEMEAT but never in PIE

My second's in HUMBLE and also in HIGH

My third's in a GRUNDY but not in a SNELL

My fourth's found in RINGING though never in BELL

My fifth's seen in SUSAN but isn't in NEIL

My sixth is in CARTER but not found in WHEEL

My seventh's not in ALDRIDGE though you'll find it in HOME

My eighth is in CRACKER but isn't in POEM

My ninth is in ARCHERS but never in QUIVER

My whole is a time that suits the good liver!

answers ➔ page 122

WHO'S THIS?

Can you fit the jigsaw pieces in the grid so that each column
spells the first name of an Ambridge villager?

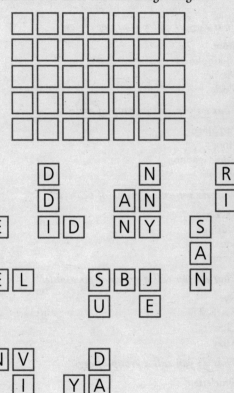

answers ➜ page 122

COUNTRYSIDE COLLECTIVES

A group of Archers at a party just has to be a quiver of Archers!
But what other country collective nouns do you know?

1 What do you call a group of crows?

a Stone
b Unkindliness
c Murder
d Flock

2 What do you call a group of owls?

a Parliament
b Hoot
c Congregation
d School

3 What do you call a group of beaters?

a Racket
b Aldridge
c Squad
d Troop

4 What do you call a group of pheasants?

a Nye
b Poached
c Cluster
d Array

5 What do you call a group of eggs?

a Omelette
b Set
c Brake
d Clutch

answers → page 123

6 What do you call a group of eels?

a Riggle
b Swarm
c Wetness
d Litter

7 What do you call a group of boars?

a River
b Cluster
c Sounder
d Room

8 What do you call a group of rabbits?

a Siffling
b Stew
c Breed
d Nest

9 What do you call a group of onions?

a Rope
b Forest
c Odour
d Prize

10 What do you call a group of peacocks?

a Garden
b Pod
c Eye
d Muster

11 What do you call a group of starlings?

a Starlet
b Murmuration
c Yoke
d Run

answers → page 123

VANISHING ACT

Rearrange the missing letters of the alphabet to spell out the first
name of a favourite Ambridge character

Oh No They Didn't!

Ambridge is not known for doing things by halves, so it's no
surprise to learn that in 1991 there were two Christmas
pantomimes. The only trouble is that both were Aladdin!
One version took place in Ambridge Hall while the other was
performed in the Village Hall. Below are two jumbled up cast
lists. The actors and directors are in the right production but they
seem to have forgotten what part they're playing.
Can you help them out?

Aladdin - Ambridge Hall

Aladdin - Nelson Gabriel
Abanazer - Lynda Snell
Princess Valroubador - Eddie Grundy
Widow Twanky - Caroline Bone
Wishee Washee - Debbie Travers-Macy

DIRECTED BY JOE GRUNDY

Aladdin - Village Hall

Aladdin - Bert Fry
Abanazer - Ruth Archer
Princess Valroubador - George Barford
Widow Twanky - Eddie Grundy
Wishee Washee - Bert Fry

DIRECTED BY KATHY PERKS

answers ➜ page 123

OUR COUNTRYSIDE'S FEATHERED FRIENDS

Tom Forrest used to introduce the Sunday omnibus with a few
seasonal words about what was going on in the countryside.
You could learn a lot listening to him but how much
do you remember?

1 The bullbat is known as . . . .

a *Shires cricketer*
b *Little owl*
c *Night hawk*
d *Black guillemot*
e *Night elf*

2 The dunnock is also called . . . .

a *Twinned partridge*
b *Wren*
c *House sparrow*
d *Hedge sparrow*
e *Heron*

3 The black cap is known as . . . .

a *Coverdale*
b *Great tit*
c *Judge*
d *Priest*
e *Monk*

answers ➜ page 123

4 The lapwing has two other names – what are they?

a *Spitfire*
b *Northern robin*
c *Peewit*
d *Green plover*
e *Linnet*

5 What two other names does the goldcrest have?

a *Greater spotted loxley*
b *Woodcock pilot*
c *Golden crested wren*
d *Gold tit*
e *Little eagle*

6 What is another name for the wood pigeon?

a *The cooee bird*
b *January warbler*
c *Cushat*
d *The piebird*
e *Cushion*

7 What is another name for the song thrush?

a *Kathy*
b *Martha*
c *Mavis*
d *Edna*
e *Clarrie*

answers → page 123

WORDSEARCH

UNHEARD OF AMBRIDGE

You may never have heard them – but can you see them? Here are
the clues to the words you'll find in the Wordsearch, reading
horizontally, vertically, diagonally and backwards. (You can also find
the solutions to the clues upside-down at the foot of the page). Spot
the hidden word that describes them (7). Good luck!

Nelson's invaluable associate and 'queen of quiche' (5)

Kenton's estranged wife (3,6)

Grey Gables' Assistant Manager, with acting ambitions (5,6)

Leading light in the Pony Club, and a twinkle in Brian's eye (5,11)

One of Eddie Grundy's disreputable friends (5)

Another of Eddie's disreputable friends (6)

Bert's stalwart wife and a dab hand at pastry (5,3)

Jack Woolley's enigmatic chauffeur (4,5)

Eddie's dancing partner for Disco Diggers (3,4)

Head Gardener at Lower Loxley (8)

Anonymous letter writer who lives at the Glebelands (5,8)

Strong supporter of local events, with weak bladder (2,6)

Housekeeper at Lower Loxley (3,7)

Lady Goodman's first name (8)

Former cook at Cat & Fiddle who now works at Lower Loxley (4)

answers ➔ page 124

```
G S O Y W E N L U L P M B E N W N T
R E H C T E L F K E R E D O C T R I
U G P A R O A R T I T O M J Z O S M
O S U C U T C T R U D Y P O R T E R
F R A H P Y W U E S R I B H S I E G
S L C A F O S A B M T M T N E P B T
E P U M L H I Y R E U A G H E D U I
B L R A D Y G P D F B N E I L L P T
E A Y L A S U E O L G D T G S S N C
B O T S H L R Q H P U Y G G A B F O
M L W O L K T E Y M S B H S L R E M
C A U E A X M R M E O E T A R E D B
T C N O S E F B V L L E R S H A N E
O S Y H J A R A I A G S U K K W Z G
M B S V D N D M T R H B G H S I S P
E E O E F R E K D C G O S U L U J T
S B R N Y O N H E H M R Y O P E I Y
H F G C A P S C I E A O N R N S N D
E L I H E O H T A R D U W M T O R A
N E S G O D U A M Y P G V E T C O M
A T K O H J E N A U L H Y B N I U G
B E C N E L I S F Y A E D R F T H T
```

answers ➜ page 124

XMAS CRACKER TEASERS

Can you sort out the jumbled up words below
and put them in the correct order?
Then see if you can work out which character said what!

1 good and banned you're time for this it's Eddie

a Ed making up a song for Dross

b Clarrie waiting on her wedding day

c Sid Perks getting angry with a customer

d Debbie performing in a village panto

2 !eee-coo

a George Barford doing a bird impression

b Eccles the resident Bull peacock

c Greg Turner on a pheasant shoot

d Jennifer Aldridge popping round to see a neighbour

3 beauty pal hello me old old me

a Ruth Archer talking to a cow

b Walter Gabriel greeting a good friend

c Jack Woolley singing in the bath

d Brian Aldridge admiring his reflection in the mirror

4 !noooo - ooh

a Lynda Snell treading in something nasty

b Tom Archer tasting Helen's organic cheese

c Neil Carter sliding down the church bell rope

d Ruth Archer taken by an unpleasant surprise

5 everyday an folk of story country

a Ruth and David Archer describing their life's journey

b Jennifer Aldridge discussing her archive project

c Radio announcer introducing a Light programme

d Lynda Snell advertising one of her plays

answers → page 124

SECRET SANTA!

Take two consecutive letters from each of the three words on a
line to form a six letter word. For instance, DISC RILE RAPT
would mean someone got a script for Christmas!

Write the letters in the grid below to find out what treats are in
Santa's sack for good little Archers.

David	SIGN	OMEN	NEST
Ruth	INCA	HOME	RAKE
Nigel	ALFA	TALC	GONE
Elizabeth	CARD	HAND	LEEK
Jennifer	BRAT	HOOT	ARCH
Brian	BOOT	OXEN	CARS

David			
Ruth			
Nigel			
Elizabeth			
Jennifer			
Brian			

answers → page 125

CHRISTMAS AT THE BULL – PUB QUIZ CHARITY SPECIAL!

Sid: 'Good evening, ladies and gentlemen, and welcome to The Bull's Christmas special. As usual you can do this as teams or on your own. I see we have Grundys, Carters, Tuckers, Frys and Barfords. Any more takers? My lovely lady wife here will be umpire and her decision is final. I hope you've bought plenty of raffle tickets because it's all for a good cause. Right, let's get started, heads down and no cheating!'

Jolene: 'I've got my eye on you, Eddie Grundy ....'

ROUND ONE

'Bert Fry should do well on this one!
Complete these country couplets'

1 *Red sky in morning shepherd's warning.*
   Red sky at night . . . ?
2 *Oak before ash, shall have a splash*
   Ash before oak . . . ?
3 *Rain before seven, shine . . . ?*
4 *Ice in November will bear a duck.*
   February weather all mire . . . ?
5 *Between twelve and two you'll see . . . ?*

ROUND TWO

'What kind of birds or animals are these? George Barford knows his birds so he's in with a chance!'

1 *Chester White, Hampshire, Tamworth, Middle White?*
2 *Spotted, Fell, Welsh, Shetland?*
3 *Muscovy, Indian Runner, Aylesbury?*
4 *Golden Guernsey, British Toggenbury, Saanen?*
5 *Dexter, South Devon, Simmental?*

answers → page 125

ROUND THREE

'Know your neighbour! Let's see what you lot really know about Ambridge!'

1 Who lives at Willow Farm?
2 Who owns eight acres at Willow Farm, where he keeps his pigs?
3 Who worked for Nelson in his Wine Bar and had a collection of autographed celebrity photos?
4 Where did Tim and Siobhan Hathaway live together?
5 Where did Clarrie Grundy live before she married?

ROUND FOUR

'Who's Who? Yes, Mrs Aldridge, we know you're in it!'

1 Who married the Aldridge's German au pair, Eva Lenz?
2 What is the name of Julia Pargetter's younger sister?
3 Who did Duncan Gemmell marry in 1994?
4 Who led the armed raid on the Ambridge post office?
5 What was the first name of Mrs Antrobus's husband?

ROUND FIVE

'Local Knowledge – Where's what?
(and no Joe, the Little Drummer Boy isn't a pub!)'

1 The ghost of the 'Little Drummer Boy'
2 The Goat & Nightgown pub
3 Ambridge's nearest railway station
4 Underwoods
5 The largest farm house in Ambridge

answers ➜ page 125

ROUND SIX

'Right, this one's about occupations. Still trying to find one, Eddie?'

1   What did Arthur (Doughy) Hood do?
2   What is Cyril Hood's job?
3   Who is the head gamekeeper for the Home Farm Estate shoot?
4   What does Wayne Foley do?
5   Who was the Vicar of Ambridge from January 1989–December1990?

ROUND SEVEN

'Here you go, Phil, country lore – something for you! Complete the following proverbs.'

1   Let sleeping dogs . . . ?
2   His bark is worse than . . . ?
3   If wishes were horses, beggars . . . ?
4   Even a worm . . . ?
5   You can't make silk purse out of . . . ?

ROUND EIGHT

'Right, Brian, you can tell a buck from a doe! - What do you call the following?'

1   A male goat
2   A young deer
3   A male sheep
4   A female horse
5   A male duck

answers ➔ page 126

ROUND NINE

'Ok then, we know we don't all originally come from Ambridge but have you any idea about where your neighbours come from?'

1 Which county does Ruth Archer come from?
2 Who comes from Stirchley, Birmingham?
3 Brian and Jennifer's au pair, Eva Lenz, (Eddie be quiet!) came from which country?
4 Which county does George Barford come from?
5 Which couple moved to Ambridge from Sunningdale in 1986?

ROUND TEN

'Well Ambridge has been a host to certain well-known people over the years. See if you can guess who these are!'

1 Which celebrity faced a challenge when she was enlisted to help refurbish the village hall?
2 Which Irish celebrity took part in a golf match at Grey Gables in 1989?
3 Which gardening celebrity gave the ladies something to talk about in 2003?
4 Which well known Radio 1 DJ was given some demo tapes by Eddie Grundy to listen to?
5 Which aristocratic twosome attended a fashion show at Grey Gables in 1984?

'Thank you one and all. Mark your papers and give them to Jolene here, buy yourselves a drink or three and we'll let you know who's won in half an hour!'

answers → page 126

GRANGE FARM AND THE GRUNDYS

Christmas is a time of plenty but as we enjoy our piled plates of roast turkey, let us pause awhile to think of the poor.
The name Grundy springs to mind. The Grundys know all about scraping a living from the soil and being pushed around by the Archer family. In 1999 they spent their last Christmas at Grange Farm, their much loved family home. By April of that same year they were bankrupt and had been evicted.

What else do you know about this sad struggling Ambridge family?

1 Who evicted the Grundys?

2 What was Joe Grundy armed with when he took up sentry duty in the yard in January 2000?

3 What was discovered on Grange Farm land in 1995?

a Remains of a dinosaur
b Joe's grandfather's teeth
c Remains of a German plane
d A Roman helmet

4 What did Clarrie win in 1993?

a A Do It Yourself book
b The Miss Borsetshire Contest
c A working holiday on a farm
d A luxury bathroom

5 What misfortune happened at Grange Farm in 1996?

a Joe was offered a full time job
b The milking parlour was destroyed by fire
c Clarrie went on a three month strike
d All the crops failed

answers → page 126

6 What happened to Brian Aldridge at Grange Farm in 1989?

ⓐ He was hurt while pushing Joe out the way of a cow with BSE
ⓑ He was accidentally shot
ⓒ He got locked in the turkey shed
ⓓ He was slapped by Clarrie for taking liberties

7 What is the first name of Joe Grundy's wife?

8 Who is William's godmother?

9 What animal lost its life during the Grange Farm Fire?

10 Who is the assistant gamekeeper for the Estate shoot?

11 Who was Eddie and Clarrie's best man at their wedding?

12 What was the name of William Grundy's pedigree Jersey cow?

ⓐ Daisy   ⓑ Cinnamon
ⓑ Becks   ⓓ Posh Spice

13 What is the name of the band that Ed plays in?

ⓐ Noise   ⓑ Mash
ⓒ Dross   ⓓ Rubbish

14 What complaint does Joe suffer from?

ⓐ Farmer's Cough   ⓑ Farmer's Lung
ⓒ Mange   ⓓ Idleitus

15 Who was Eddie once set to marry?

ⓐ Debbie Travers-Macy   ⓑ Jolene Perks
ⓒ Mandy Beesborough   ⓓ Dolly Treadgold

16 Where did Clarrie want to move to?

ⓐ France
ⓑ Isle of Man
ⓒ Wales
ⓓ Anywhere with a built-in dishwasher

answers ➜ page 126

THE AMBRIDGESHOOT
QUICK FIRE ROUND

A quick fire round to test your general knowledge of *The Archers*.
The first answer you give must count as the final one
and you must finish the quiz in 2 minutes!
Remember – you have only one shot at each question!
Get ready – finger on the trigger – GO!

1 Who owns the Village Shop?

2 What is Bert Fry's wife called?

3 Who abandoned Elizabeth Archer during a journey
  on the M40?

4 With which doctor did Caroline Bone move in in 1987?

5 Who was abandoned by Clive Horrobin with a six week
  old baby?

6 Which ice-cream seller was known as Mr Snowy?

7 Which ice-cream seller was known as Mrs Snowy?

8 Who originally came from Kampala in Uganda?

9 What was Hayley Tucker's maiden name?

10 What was the name of Simon Pemberton's father?

11 What is the name of Sid and Kathy Perks' son?

12 Who killed ferrets with a lump hammer?

13 What was the name of The Bull's rival pub?

14 What was the maiden name of George Barford's wife?

answers ➔ page 126

15 What is Philippa Rose Archer's nickname?

16 What is the name of Jack Woolley's chauffeur?

17 What is the name of Sid Perks' daughter by his first wife, Polly?

18 Who is Kenton Archer's twin?

19 Who was Clarrie Grundy's father?

20 Who was killed in a tractor accident in 1998?

Now check your answers on page 126 to discover how many pheasants you can take home in your hamper!

'DECK THE HALLS'

As Lynda sits sipping mulled wine she takes a look at the bright and fragrant plants and shrubs she's used to decorate Ambridge Hall. See if you can fit the winter plants listed below into the grid so that the shaded diagonal spells out the centrepiece of a traditional festive display . . .

CYCLAMEN, POINSETTIA, MISTELTOE, NARCISSUS, AMARYLLIS, JASMINE, WINTERCHERRY, AZALEA

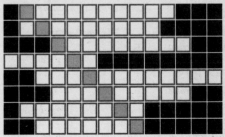

answers ➔ page 127

THEY SEEK THEM HERE, THEY SEEK THEM THERE

Can you fit these Ambridge locations into the grid?

7 LETTERS
The Bull

8 LETTERS
Home Farm

9 LETTERS
Lakey Hill

10 LETTERS
Brookfield   *Dower House*
Grange Farm   *Grey Gables*
St Stephen's   *The Stables*
Willow Farm

11 LETTERS
Lower Loxley   *Village Shop*

12 LETTERS
Ambridge Hall   *Glebe Cottage*
Heydon Berrow

14 LETTERS
Lyttleton Brook

15 LETTERS
Nightingale Farm

answers ➜ page 122

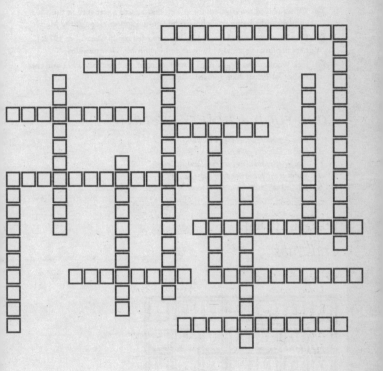

answers → page 122

SOLUTIONS

SEASONS GREETINGS

1 *c* After the family gave a rousing version of Auld Lang Syne, Dan uttered the immortal words 'And a Happy New Year to all'. It was the first national broadcast of *The Archers* !

2 *b* Walter played the euphonium so well that he was a star turn at the annual carol-singing party hosted by Squire Lawson-Hope at the Manor.

3 *d* Joby Woodford and Martha Lily were married on 25 December 1972. Mrs Perkins was maid of honour and Canon Meridew presided.

4 *b* Jack Woolley and Peggy Archer were married on 1 January 1991 and the Bishop of Felpersham himself officiated.

GOOD FOOD & HEARTY CHEER

1 c *John Archer produced organic pork.*
2 d *Brian Aldridge got drunk on Calvados.*
3 c *The Grey Gables chef is Jean-Paul Aubert.*
4 d *Shires is the favourite drink at The Bull.*
5 b *Joe Grundy added a lump of meat to his home-brewed cider.*

RIDDLE ME REE

Christmas

WHO'S THIS?

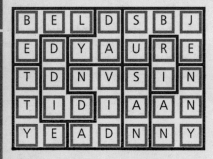

COUNTRYSIDE COLLECTIVES

1 *c* Murder of crows

2 *a* Parliament of owls

3 *c* Squad of beaters

4 *a* Nye of pheasants

5 *d* Clutch of eggs

6 *b* Swarm of eels

7 *c* Sounder of boars

8 *d* Nest of rabbits

9 *a* Rope of onions

10 *d* Muster of peacocks

11 *b* Murmuration of starlings

VANISHING ACT

Answer: Lynda

Lynda Snell has fine-tuned her ability to irritate all Ambridge villagers in turn. However her heart is in the right place and Ambridge would be the poorer without her.

OH YES THEY DID!

Aladdin - Ambridge Hall	Aladdin - Village Hall
Aladdin - Debbie Aldridge	Aladdin - Ruth Archer
Abanazer - Joe Grundy	Abanazer - Bert Fry
Princess Valroubador - Caroline Bone	Princess Valroubador - Kathy Perks
Widow Twanky - Nelson Gabriel	Widow Twanky - George Barford
Wishee Washee - Eddie Grundy	Wishee Washee - Eddie Grundy
DIRECTED BY LYNDA SNELL	DIRECTED BY BERT FRY

Eddie played Wishee Washee in both productions and Bert Fry directed and took part in the Village Hall production

OUR COUNTRYSIDE FEATHERED FRIENDS

1 *c* Night hawk

2 *d* Hedge sparrow

3 *e* Monk

4 *c* and *d* Peewit and green plover

5 *b* and *c* Woodcock pilot and Golden crested wren

6 *c* Cushat

7 *c* Mavis

WORDSEARCH – UNHEARD OF AMBRIDGE

The secret word is SILENCE!

R	E	H	C	T	E	L		F	K	E	R	E	D				
						A							J				
			T			T	R	U	D	Y	P	O	R	T	E	R	
			P								H						
		A				M		M		N						T	
	U				R			A		H					I		
L				P				N		I					T		
			U					D		G					C		
		L						Y	G	G	A	B			O		
			L		Y	M		B		S					M		
	E			R		E		E							B		
N					F		L	L	E		S	H	A	N	E		
		A					A		S								
M		D				R		B	G								
E	E					C		O		U							
R				H		H		R			P						
F	C			C		E		O				S					
E			E	T		R		U	W				R			M	
	D			A			G		E								
		E	N			H			N								
E	C	N	E	L	I	S											

XMAS CRACKER TEASERS

1 You're banned Eddie and this time it's for good

   c) Sid Perks getting angry with a customer

   Over the years Eddie Grundy was frequently banned from The Bull but he was always able to take refuge at The Cat & Fiddle. Now that pub's closed he seems to behave a little better!

2 Coo-eee!

   d) Jennifer Aldridge popping round to see a neighbour

   Jennifer's piping 'Coo-eee' has presaged all sorts of scenes between her and her family and friends. Recently it looks as if Lynda Snell has decided to get it on the act – but she can only ever be an understudy.

3 Hello me old pal me old beauty

   b) Walter Gabriel greeting a good friend

   This simply must be the classic Archers catch-phrase of all time.

4 **OOH- noooo!**

    (d) Ruth Archer taken by an unpleasant surprise

        Dead Ringers have made this endearing catchphrase famous.

5 **An everyday story of country folk**

    (c) Radio announcer introducing a famous Light programme

        A description of what The Archers used to be about that is guaranteed to make the more seasoned listener sigh with nostalgia!

SECRET SANTA

Santa gave David gnomes (a Grundy Santa by any chance?), Ruth a camera (for her spare time), Nigel a falcon (in case Eleanor escapes again), Elizabeth a candle with a relaxing fragrance (so she can chill out away from the children), Jennifer a brooch (no doubt encrusted with jewels) and Brian a pair of boxers (now who was responsible for that?).

CHRISTMAS AT THE BULL

Round One

1 *Red sky at night, shepherd's delight*
2 *Ash before oak, we shall have a soak.*
3 *Rain before seven, shine before eleven*
4 *February weather, all mire and muck*
5 *Between twelve and two you'll see what the day will do.*

Round Two

1 Pigs	2 Ponies	3 Ducks
4 Goats	5 Cattle	

Round Three

1 The Tuckers	2 Neil Carter	3 Shane
4 Honeysuckle Cottage	5 Woodbine Cottage	

Round Four

1 PC James Coverdale (now Detective Inspector)	2 Ellen Rogers
3 Lucy Perks	4 Clive Horrobin	5 Edward or 'Teddy'

Round Five

1 The Bull	2 Borchester (near the Tech)
3 Hollerton Junction	4 Borchester (a department store)
5 Home Farm	

Round Six

1 Arthur Hood was a baker 2 Cyril Hood is the Bishop of Felpersham.
3 Greg Turner   4 Wayne Foley has his own show on Radio Borsetshire.
5 Jeremy Buckle (Jerry)

WINTER

Round Seven

1	lie	2	bite	3	would ride
4	will turn	5	a sow's ear		

Round Eight

1	Billy goat or ram	2	Fawn	3	Ram
4	Mare	5	Drake		

Round Nine

1	Northumberland	2	Jack Woolley	3	Germany
4	Yorkshire	5	Lynda and Robert Snell		

Round Ten

1	Anneka Rice	2	Terry Wogan	3	Alan Titchmarsh
4	John Peel	5	HRH Princess Margaret and The Duke of Westminster		

GRANGE FARM AND THE GRUNDYS

1   Borchester Land evicted the Grundys.

2   Joe was armed with a shotgun.

3   *c* The remains of a German plane

4   *d* A luxury bathroom

5   *b* The milking parlour was destroyed by fire.

6   *a* Brian got hurt pushing Joe out of the way of a cow with BSE.

7   Joe's wife's first name was Susan.

8   Caroline Pemberton is William's godmother.

9   Gyp, Jethro Larkin's old collie, died in the Grange Farm fire.

10   William Grundy is Assistant Gamekeeper for the Estate Shoot.

11   Alf Grundy was best man at Eddie and Clarrie's wedding.

12   *d* Posh Spice was the name of William's Jersey cow.

13   *c* Dross is the name of the band Ed plays in.

14   *b* Joe suffers from Farmer's Lung.

15   *d* Eddie Grundy nearly married Dolly Treadgold.

16   *a* Clarrie wanted to move to France.

THE AMBRIDGE SHOOT QUICK FIRE ROUND

1	Jack Woolley	2	Freda Fry	3	Cameron Fraser
4	Dr Matthew Thorogood	5	Sharon Richards	6	Nigel Pargetter
7	Elizabeth Archer	8	Usha Gupta	9	Hayley Jordan
10	Guy Pemberton	11	Jamie Perks	12	Joe Grundy
13	The Cat & Fiddle	14	Christine Archer	15	Pip
16	John Higgs	17	Lucy Gemmell	18	Shula Hebden Lloyd
19	Jethro Larkin	20	John Archer		

20 correct answers. Congratulations – you are the Brain of Borsetshire! You are well able to hold your own with the Archers, Aldridges or Woolleys! Three brace of pheasants and a bottle of Bollinger for you.

15–19 correct answers. Excellent. Well up to the standard of the Lloyds, Pembertons and Mrs Antrobus. Two brace of pheasants and a bottle of port for you.

10–15 correct answers. Not bad at all. You could have a good time with the Carters, Tuckers and Perks. One brace of pheasants and a bottle of Beaujolais for you.

0–5 correct answers. Oh dear! Is your name Grundy by any chance? A pigeon and a bottle of lemonade for you.

DECK THE HALLS

POINSETTIA
MISTLETOE
NARCISSUS
AZALEA
WINTERCHERRY
AMARYLLIS
CYCLAMEN
JASMINE

THEY SEEK THEM HERE THEY SEEK THEM THERE

Did you find them?

AMBRIDGEHALL
HEYDONBERROW
LAKEYHILL
THEBULL
GLEBECOTTAGE
VILLAGESHOP
HOMEFARM
DOWERHOUSE
LOWERLOXLEY

GREYGARGES
GRANGEFARM
SLEEPHANDS
NIGHTINGALEFARM
BROOKFIELD
WILLOWFARM
THESTABLEORBROOK
LYTTLETONBROOK